From humble beginnings Lianne Murphy has worked hard to achieve great accomplishment and success in her career as a lawyer and as a professional businesswoman. Lianne always believed that achieving her goals would bring happiness but, having exceeded even her own expectations, she recognised that she still had a limited sense of satisfaction and happiness. When her mother astonished her oncology team by living well and with great contentment for years, despite having been diagnosed with a terminal illness and a 6-month life expectancy purely as a result of focused change to her diet and lifestyle, Lianne started to explore the concept of holistic health, wellbeing and happiness in earnest. This made her wonder—what if we applied this kind of focus to our wellbeing before we became sick? What if wellness and contentment were the goals rather than chasing success and achievement? What if we started living in happiness right now rather than making it conditional upon some other life event? A deep dive of exploration into wellness followed. Lianne emerged years later with a true understanding of how to create a healthy balance in life and how to achieve a deep and lasting sense of satisfaction. From a desire to share what she had learned to help others, this book was born.

For Mum,

The discovery continues…

xxx

Lianne Murphy

BALANCE

AUSTIN MACAULEY PUBLISHERS™

LONDON • CAMBRIDGE • NEW YORK • SHARJAH

Copyright © Lianne Murphy 2024

The right of Lianne Murphy to be identified as author of this work has been asserted by the author in accordance with sections 77 and 78 of the Copyright, Designs and Patents Act 1988.

All rights reserved. No part of this publication may be reproduced, stored in a retrieval system, or transmitted in any form or by any means, electronic, mechanical, photocopying, recording, or otherwise, without the prior permission of the publishers.

Any person who commits any unauthorised act in relation to this publication may be liable to criminal prosecution and civil claims for damages.

A CIP catalogue record for this title is available from the British Library.

ISBN 9781398415829 (Paperback)
ISBN 9781398415836 (Hardback)
ISBN 9781398415843 (ePub e-book)

www.austinmacauley.com

First Published 2024
Austin Macauley Publishers Ltd®
1 Canada Square
Canary Wharf
London
E14 5AA

Thanks go to:

My beautiful family, for encouraging me to write this book and for providing the best ever reason for learning to live well;

Aunty Pop, thank you for believing in me and for seeing the goodness in me, even before I could see it in myself.

Michelle, my business partner, proof reader, teacher and most importantly my dear friend, our connection is one of my most treasured blessings.

Paulette, I have valued your support, wisdom, encouragement and guidance so much.

Thank you.

Table of Contents

Introduction: What Is Wellbeing Anyway?	**13**
Chapter 1: Begin at the Beginning	**18**
Chapter 2: The Baggage of Life	**27**
Chapter 3: The Importance of Making Space	**41**
Owning our environment	*51*
Chapter 4: Setting Your Satnav	**53**
Reflection	*61*
Chapter 5: The Mind, Body and Spirit as One Moving Part	**62**
The Science	*68*
Reflection	*72*
Chapter 6: Love	**74**
Community Resilience	*75*
Physical connection	*76*
Self-care and self-love	*77*
Unconscious Absorption	*81*

Love and kindness	*84*
Connection to all things	*85*
Taking care of the heart	*86*
Loving what we have	*88*
Reflection	*89*
Chapter 7: Mindfulness	**91**
How to start living more mindfully	*94*
Mindfulness Exercise	*99*
Breathing Exercises	*100*
Chapter 8: Breathing for Beginners	**102**
Dulling pain	*104*
Improved blood flow	*104*
Increasing energy levels	*105*
Detoxification	*105*
Improving posture	*105*
Stimulating lymphatic system	*105*
Improving digestion	*106*
Activation of the parasympathetic nervous system	*106*
Exercise	*108*
Reflection	*109*
Chapter 9: Sleep Stories	**110**
Sleep Deprivation and Cognitive Function	*113*
Sleep Deprivation and Mental Health	*115*

Sleep Deprivation and Physical Health	*117*
Stimulants	*120*
Sugar	*122*
Screens	*123*
The Circadian Rhythm	*123*
Sleep and Brain Restoration	*125*
The Science	*126*
The Effect of Short Sleep on the Brain	*127*
How to get better sleep	*129*
Chapter 10: Fuel	**133**
Sugar	*138*
Processed food	*140*
Probiotics	*142*
Prebiotics	*143*
Food as medicine	*143*
Antibiotics	*146*
Hormones in food	*147*
Plastic consumption	*148*
Chemicals in daily life	*149*
Meat	*150*
Soya	*153*
Carbs	*154*
Alcohol	*157*

Supplements	*158*
Hydration	*161*
Chapter 11: Mind	**164**
Chapter 12: Body	**182**
Chapter 13: Soul	**194**
Chapter 14: The Next Generation	**201**
Epilogue	**206**

Introduction
What Is Wellbeing Anyway?

The Oxford English Dictionary defines wellbeing as "the state of being comfortable, healthy or happy." As each of us strives to achieve a greater sense of wellbeing in our lives, it is helpful to understand how our bodies and minds work together to create this state of wellness and how to maintain it.

In the stressful and fast paced modern world, many of us have become disconnected with what it really means to feel well. It has somehow become increasingly difficult to justify prioritising our own needs above our responsibilities of our career, family, home environment and so on. We become used to the daily grind and normalise our feelings of stress and a lack of fulfilment. Our focus becomes narrowed and we start to miss out on the enjoyment of what surrounds us. We stop questioning our path in life. We stop reviewing the course that we are following to make sure that it is still taking us where we want to go.

Wellbeing is a question of review and balance. We must stop and check our charted course and also ensure that our ship is balanced. We should also make sure that we are still enjoying the ride!

Our mind, body and soul are absolutely and deeply enmeshed; it is not possible to achieve true wellbeing without all three being in a state of wellness and balance. The ultimate aim for most of us is to achieve comfort, peace and fulfilment in life and to reach our potential. This book is designed to help to identify which areas might be in need of attention and to offer support in making the changes necessary to move towards a sense of genuine and meaningful happiness.

The challenge for most of us in the modern world is finding the time to stand still for long enough to realise what does need to be changed. We never realise how tired we truly are because what we eat and drink conceals it; we never realise how much our bodies need a break because we are so used to living with the aches, pains and stiffness that have slowly developed over years of running around; we have no concept of how stress is impacting upon our health because stress is the norm and also because a mind in a state of stress is unable to properly identify stress! It is a perfect storm. There comes a time for all of us when we reach the eye of that storm. Something makes us stop and think about whether we are happy; causes us to re-evaluate our purpose and reorganise our priorities. Often it is something catastrophic such as; bereavement or a diagnosis of ill health in us or a loved one that makes us stop and think. It may also be after achieving something that we have strived for, for years, something that we believed would bring us happiness and when we actually reach our goal, we realise that happiness is nowhere to be found. In these reflective moments, there is opportunity for change. It is absolutely possible to come out the other side and into the sunshine. It is absolutely possible to reframe our lives, to identify what brings meaning and fulfilment.

The concept of wellbeing can be applied to any part of our life which holds possibility for change and improvement. This can include mental health, physical health, being connected with a sense of purpose, nutrition, stress management, happiness, sleep patterns and so on. The concept of wellness is entirely subjective; it is completely unique to each of us as individuals. Each of us has had different life experiences and have developed different patterns and habits to manage how we live, feel and work. It follows then that we will each need to tweak a different element of our lifestyle to achieve the desired improvement and to increase the feel-good factor in our lives. It is likely that each of us will be prepared to commit to a different degree or to varying timescales for change to increase that sense of wellness and, of course, that may fluctuate over time. Wellbeing of the individual is an entirely holistic and bespoke concept. To achieve wellness in mind, body and spirit is a challenge but will pay the investment back, ten-fold. Finding the elusive balance between those elements is essential to being able to maintain it. This book will provide a deeper understanding of what underpins our health, so enabling greater success in achieving and maintaining our goals.

As with all change, reframing habits and how we live and think takes courage and commitment and can be tough at times. Taking proper care of ourselves during that process is key to being able to continue when the challenges arise. Positive self-care is the first step to feeling good and being able to take proper care of others. Remember the rule about fitting our own oxygen mask first before trying to help anyone else? It applies to everything. A journey into self-care and being kind to ourselves in everything that we do will pay dividends in our quest for change for the better.

This book will help you to grow in so many ways; outwards in confidence, upwards in strength and more deeply rooted in security and self-esteem. Life is rarely always easy for any of us but it is the storms that make us stronger. This book will guide you to develop confidence in yourself and in the core well-being principle that when your roots grow deeply and your stature is strong, there is no need whatsoever to fear the wind and the rain.

Join the ALTR Life Lifestyle Revolution...

Worship Yourself: Create Change

How to use this book:

Each chapter is overflowing with information about self-care, health and well-being. There is no need to read it in order and if there is a particular topic of interest to you then dive right in! The chapters don't repeat the medical explanations and scientific background that is dealt with in earlier chapters, however. Many of the chapters contain a section called 'The Science' which is a little more technical than the rest. Again, it is not completely necessary to read these sections but doing so will improve your understanding of how your body and mind function, which should help you to understand how to take good care of it all.

At the end of each chapter, there is a mantra. If you are using meditative, gratitude or mindfulness practices, these mantras will help to focus your mind to reinforce what you are reading. Taking five minutes to sit comfortably, close your eyes, using breathing exercises to relax and then repeating the mantra in your mind or out loud will positively reinforce the message that you are giving to yourself. The more you can do this, the stronger the reinforcement will be.

You will also find practical exercises that you can use to identify how beneficial it might be to spend additional time working on any specific area. Again, this does not have to be done in any particular order or before or after reading the corresponding chapter in the book. However, reading the relevant chapter will provide a deeper understanding of how the body and mind functions in this area. Having that knowledge before embarking upon the practical exercise may help you to derive greater benefit from it. Obviously, the exercises can be done more than once and you may want to complete an exercise and then read, repeating the exercise afterwards and notice how you approach it differently or whether the outcome has changed for you.

However, you use this book, one thing is certain: It will change you. That change will be for the better. Congratulations on making this investment in yourself and enjoy the ride…

Mantra: I am worthy of everything I seek

Chapter 1
Begin at the Beginning

We are each born full of opportunity and promise, life and love and purity. As we traverse the bumpy road of life with all its twists and turns, we become conditioned in so many ways. We are influenced by our habits whether consciously or subconsciously formed and by the people who surround us. We become a product of our environment. We are shaped by our cultural norms, family traditions, the expectations of society, our friendship groups and social circle. Our decision making is often unconscious and automatic. The more automation that creeps into our lives, the less mindfully we begin to live and the less we notice the treadmill that we are on, mindlessly carrying us through the years in a direction that we may never have actually consciously chosen for ourselves.

The power of choice:

The conditioning that we face in the modern world is not designed to be damaging or to negatively impact upon us. Indeed, many people happily progress through life, not even noticing that they have been or continue to be conditioned and are living a life that they did not consciously choose.

However, once we come to notice that life isn't perhaps all that we would choose for it to be, we may seek to make changes. At this stage we become aware that, in fact, we have asserted much less power and control over our own lives than we could have done.

As human beings, we are each blessed with a life of unpredictable length. Given that we never know when our time in this life will run out, why are we not running towards our wildest dreams like we are on fire? Why do we waste time on the things that do not serve us? Things that don't bring us happiness or a sense of worth or purpose? Why do we hang onto decisions that we made years ago that no longer fit? Why do we not feel empowered to live a life that is true to ourselves? Why do we prioritise the happiness of others above our own sense of self? Why do we absorb the negativity or issues of others, irrespective of the negative impact that doing so may have upon our own wellbeing? There is one answer to all of these questions which may be tough to swallow but it is absolutely and universally true. It is because we have become conditioned to think that we have no power to change it and so, by default, we have chosen to make it so.

Some may not agree with the validity of this reality but there comes a time in every life where we have to take responsibility for ourselves and the circumstances that we find ourselves in. It is, of course, the case that we do not choose the family that we are born into. We do not choose the religion or social circles that our families move in when we are growing up and which will undoubtedly influence our own development. It is also a fact that we cannot control the actions of others and, therefore, we may be subjected to experiences throughout the course of our lives, not just in our childhood that we would not have chosen for ourselves. We may not have the luxury of infinite choice because of financial circumstances or obligations and commitments such as: dependants or disability or a binding commitment. However, if we find ourselves in a situation that feels uncomfortable and if it starts to feel like it doesn't fit well then, it's time to change it. We should not feel uncomfortable in our own mind, skin, home, family, workplace, social circle, society, environment or beliefs. If we wore an uncomfortable sweater that distracted us from our day, that prevented us from having a good night's sleep, what would we do? We would wear a different sweater the next day! We certainly wouldn't wear it over and over, becoming more and more irritated or letting our skin become sore and damaged. Even if we didn't have a different sweater to wear, we would at least cut out the label out or put a T-shirt on underneath whilst we saved for a new sweater! The point is, we would make ourselves feel more comfortable and commit to change and that would be a priority for us.

Discomfort distracts us from focusing on other things and prevents us from fulfilling our potential. When we feel unsettled in ourselves, our self-esteem suffers too. We don't feel grounded, secure or safe. We make decisions which are based in discomfort and from a place of insecurity. Those decisions shape a future which keeps us held in the very same place that we feel unsettled and insecure. Breaking out of that pattern into a positive cycle of self-assurance and positive change starts with a single small step. It can be anything at all but it must be something. We must make a conscious decision to want to change, to want to improve our lot, to be open to being a different vision of ourselves. Taking that first step, that conscious decision, may feel like an impossible leap at first but it is absolutely achievable with the right mind set. We have to feel empowered to take control of our lives if we are to effect positive change.

Self-belief

Self-belief is sometimes difficult to achieve within a restrictive environment. We may feel that we are being driven by factors outside of our control, by fear, addiction, conditioning or a lack of self-confidence. We may feel that we are not strong enough to survive outside of the life that we know. We may feel that we do not deserve more than we have. Whatever trap our leg is caught in, whatever is holding us back from free choice can be set free. Whatever is holding power over our progress is only as powerful as we make it in our own minds. The key to long term and sustained positive transformation is to conquer your own mind. If we can conquer our mind, we can transform any aspect of our life into anything we choose.

Our mind-set is at the heart of everything that we do. It dictates whether we perceive our experiences as negative, destructive and disempowering or whether we can view them as learning opportunities and a chance to grow in strength, resilience and power. Mind-set controls what we expect from our day: positive or negative. Mind-set holds the boundaries of the behaviour that we are prepared to accept from others, the level at which we interact with our peers, the amount of energy that we consider to be worthy to invest in ourselves and in our development, the quality of our relationships, the degree to which we will achieve success or whether we are destined to live a life of stagnation and unhappiness. Whether you think that you are a winner or a loser, happy or sad, a success or a failure, whether you think that you can or whether you think that you can't, you are right.

What many of us fail to appreciate until much later in life is that we have control over our mind-set. It is possible to change psychological habits, even those developed over a lifetime. If we look at this theory from outside of ourselves, it becomes very simple to accept. Where does our thinking originate? From inside of ourselves, of course. Nobody can force us what to think. Our thoughts originate within our own minds and so must be capable of being controlled from within. It logically follows that the only person who can control our thought processes is ourselves! Once we accept this fact, taking control over our thinking and our mind set, even over those racing thoughts or destructive memories becomes a possibility. To make that possibility a reality, we have to choose to take control. We have to choose to make change. We have to choose to do the work that is necessary to move our thoughts in a different direction. We have to choose to keep doing that over and over until we have created new habits and strengthened our self-belief and self-control to the point where we can truly trust and have confidence in our authentic selves and the choices we make. We wouldn't expect to change our body shape without consistently making good choices about nutrition and exercise, so it is that we have to be consistent in our will to change the shape of our thinking and mind-set.

It can be done. It is achievable if we choose to commit to it.

Empowerment:

If we do not choose to make changes for ourselves then, by default, we are choosing to allow things to remain as they are. Whilst we may be travelling a path that we did not originally select, by failing to change direction at the crossroads we are making a choice to continue to walk in the same direction. At that point, we each become accountable for our environment. We can no longer blame others for the disappointment or sadness or lack of fulfilment that we feel. By blaming others for the things that we do not enjoy in our lives we give those others the power to continue to bring us down. If we choose to gift the power over our own feelings to a third party, we cannot be surprised if we feel no sense of empowerment or control to ever feel any better. We can take back that power and control by accepting that whatever has happened is in the past. We cannot control the past but we can choose the level of impact that the experience has on our present circumstances. We can make a conscious decision to confine that sadness and negativity to history and we can resolve to make our present experience a more positive one. Instead of asking 'why did this happen to me?' we can ask ourselves 'what did we learn from that experience?' Instead of asking 'why me?' we can ask 'why not me?' Instead of perceiving ourselves as the victim, we can acknowledge the strength that we demonstrated in rising up above our experience and continuing on with living. Whether we perceive ourselves as the victim or the victor, we are right. Choose to be the victor! The power to be victorious is within each of us, just waiting to celebrate.

It has to be acknowledged that some of us feel that meaningful change is impossible because of the demands of life, family, work, finances amongst so many other things. The struggles and barriers that make putting ourselves first often seem more of a dream than a reality. It is a fact that each of us will require different support with making and sustaining change. For some, it may be related to physical health and wellbeing; for others, it will be making a psychological shift or stabilising mental health and wellbeing or making space within a life that has become overwhelming. For some, support will be required in building social connections or physical strength. Some of us may need help to relax. Whatever the need, taking control of our future can provide the confidence and support required to build a purposeful and balanced life that is truly fit for living. Self-worth, self-belief and self-esteem will come from making small changes in how we look after ourselves and how we prioritise our own holistic health. It is not necessary to set ourselves on fire to keep others warm. If we encourage and develop an environment of mutual support and nurture around us, we enable everyone in that community to fulfil their potential to reach the peak of their physical, mental and spiritual fitness and in a balanced and sustainable way.

Mantras Exercise:

If you are reading this book, it is likely that you are contemplating making changes to the way you live. Whether this has been prompted by a life-changing catalyst such as: a bereavement or divorce, whether it has come from a desire to be rid of addiction or harmful behaviours, to become fitter and healthier, a simple desire to try something new or indeed one of a multitude of other possible reasons, keep this page bookmarked. Return to it whenever you are feeling like things are tough or you feel that, perhaps, it is easier to just leave things as they are. When that happens, which inevitably it will, scan your eyes over the following sentences. One will jump out at you. Repeat it (out loud if you can) ten times or with mala beads. Do this for as long or as often as you continue to feel negatively. It doesn't need to be believed, just said! By saying it often enough, the brain will start to believe it and will start to drive you in accordance with it being true. The changes and motivation to maintain it will then flow…

- I am enough
- I am worthy of my wildest dreams
- Why not me? Why not now?
- I create the change in me
- My body is stronger every day
- I can; I will; I am
- I trust and believe in who I am.
- All that I will ever need is within me.
- The victory is already mine to celebrate
- I do not have to set myself on fire to keep others warm
- I must fit my own oxygen mask before helping others
- My thoughts are mine and I control them

- This too shall pass…
- I am safe
- I have control over how I feel and I choose to feel at peace.

- I am strong, healthy and powerful
- This experience is helping me grow
- I choose to let go of what no longer serves me
- I am my problem and I am my solution
- I am present in every moment of life
- I am the healthiest version of myself
- It's my choice and I choose me

<u>Reflection:</u>

Spend some time evaluating your life balance and your goals. Look honestly at the parts of your existing life that you would not choose for yourself now. Consider how the last six months have felt, mentally, physically and emotionally and which parts you would like to change or keep the same in future. Of the things that you want to leave behind, note the one that is the most important to you. Grab a pen and write down why that is below and your plan to change it.

Mantra: I am my solution

Chapter 2
The Baggage of Life

Research shows that most of us are experiencing high levels of stress and a distorted work / life balance which negatively impacts upon our health, family or performance levels. It is completely unsustainable and every available professional recommendation is that individuals, businesses and communities take action to restore wellbeing and so improve health. Stress is a significant factor in mental health issues including anxiety and depression and is one of the great public health challenges of our time. Despite a huge surge in general acceptance and public awareness stress still isn't being taken as seriously in medical terms as physical health concerns. This is even more troubling as stress is becoming increasingly linked through clinical research to physical health issues like heart disease, problems with our immune system, insomnia, gut health and now finally to cancer.

Stress is the 'First World Problem' that must be resolved if we are to achieve a healthy and balanced existence. The modern world is riddled with stressors. A UK Mental Health Foundation study concluded that almost three quarters (74%) of UK adults had felt so stressed at some point in the preceding year that they felt overwhelmed or were unable to cope.

An American study of the impact of daily stress upon health and mood found that there was a significant relationship between daily stress and the occurrence of more common physical health problems such as: flu, sore throat, headaches and back ache. Mood disturbance was confirmed as an immediate side effect of stressful day to day living. What surprised the researchers was the extent to which the impact of daily stress was affected by different external influences and other personal factors. Those with unsupportive social relationships and low self-esteem were more likely to experience an increase in the whole spectrum of health and mood issues in response to stress than participants with high self-esteem and social support. Their resilience was significantly depleted. The importance of support and good self-esteem cannot, therefore, be underestimated in the journey towards wellbeing, particularly when managing everyday stress.

The relationship between stress and illness is complex. Susceptibility to stress varies from person to person. An event that causes an illness in one person may not cause illness in another. Events must interact with a wide variety of background factors within our bodies to become an illness. Amongst the factors that influence our susceptibility to stress are genetic vulnerability, coping style, type of personality and social support. When we are confronted with a problem, our brains are trained to assess the seriousness of the problem and to determine whether or not we have the resources necessary to cope with it. If we believe that the problem is serious and do not have the resources necessary to cope, so we will perceive ourselves as being under stress. So it is our individual way of reacting to any given situation that makes a difference in our susceptibility to illness and our overall well-being. This is entirely under our control.

Behavioural responses to stress:

Stress can cause changes in our behaviour which in turn can have a negative effect on our physical and mental health and indeed on our relationships. Difficulties sleeping are a prime example. As sleep becomes disturbed through worry and anxiety, our bodies, minds and resilience suffer too. Distraction during the waking day combined with tiredness can often contribute to an increased likelihood of accidents or irritation and a short temper.

Comfort food is often used as a way to achieve a quick 'feel good factor' and over indulgence can often be a response to a stressful situation. Unfortunately, this food is high in fat, salt and sugar, over consumption of which has been linked to depression and anxiety and which if consumed regularly over time can lead to problems with obesity, inflammation, blood pressure, diabetes and chronic disease. Managing stress with food to regain a sense of control can leading to eating disorders such as bulimia or anorexia nervosa.

Excessive behaviour is also a reliable sign of stress. Often, the use of alcohol, prescription or illegal drugs provide what appears to be a 'quick fix' to take the edge off of the difficult feelings of dysregulation that stress provokes. Use of addictive substances can quickly move to dependence, leading to associated physical and emotional issues. Other social indicators of high stress levels include withdrawal from life and social situations, exhaustion, poor timekeeping and absenteeism from work. These responses take their toll on mental health as social support networks and community resources become unavailable to lean on and normal life disappears.

Sudden risk taking behaviour is a clear sign of stress as our individual sense of worth reduces and we begin to seek a dopamine hit in feelings of enjoyment and excitement to compensate. As this coping strategy progresses, it can become harder and harder to get the 'buzz' of excitement needed to offset the stress and so we begin to take bigger and bigger risks to achieve it. Reckless driving or gambling is a common example. Unfortunately, in some cases, the sense of worthlessness becomes too much to bear and thoughts of self-harm can materialise.

Shock and trauma:

There are alternative stress responses to Cannons method of fight or flight, including to withdraw, pull back and conserve energy and also to 'tend and befriend', which is common among women and means to seek and give support. The method of withdraw, pull back and then conserve energy is most often seen after the death of a loved one or other shock or trauma. In these circumstances, most people withdraw from the situation in a state of shock. To process what has happened they pull away from the situation and display emotional responses such as crying. The last element of this stress response is the conservation of energy. This includes lying down or the stillness which often accompanies the end of crying frantically. The 'tend and befriend' method most commonly occurs with women as a reaction to high levels of stress. Women more often seek social support than men during challenging times which is considered to be extremely helpful strategy in successful stress management. Statistically, women are associated with lower instances of stress related physical illness, too. This may be explained in part by their willingness to seek support and to process difficult life events at the time they occur.

During a period of high stress 'fight or flight response' the body experiences a surge of energy which, at the end of the high stress event, is no longer required. In nature we see other species physically 'shake off' the latent energy that has built up in the body. As humans we are conditioned to revert to 'normal' behaviour as quickly as possible so leaving the energy generated by the high stress event 'stuck' within. Other stress and memories can trigger the trapped energy later on, causing long term physical and psychological effects from an earlier event.

High stress life events and modern living can cause our adrenal, endocrine, immune and nervous systems to become dysfunctional and exhausted. Over time, our failure to fully recover from significant negative events and experiences can cause impairments to proper brain development. It can prevent our bodies and minds from learning the natural and healthy physiological and psychological way to heal. In short, a failure to recover fully from high stress life events can cause life long physical and mental health issues. This book will explain the link between emotional, physical health and our environment and the perils of disconnecting them.

The link between stress and mental health:

Stress in itself is not an illness but there are connections between stress and mental health conditions including depression, anxiety, psychosis and post-traumatic stress disorder (PTSD). Some of the emotional and behavioural symptoms of stress overlap with those of mental health conditions like anxiety or depression. This can make it hard to distinguish where one begins and the other ends or which came first. When we are stressed, we may feel worried, in low mood, unable to concentrate or make decisions, irritable and angry. Chronic (or long term) stress increases the risk of developing long standing depression and anxiety in some people. The precise mechanisms of how stress is linked to mental ill-health are being uncovered but the evidence is now undeniable: the two are inextricably linked.

The Science:

Within seconds of perceiving a 'stressor', the body release chemicals which signal between nerve cells (neurotransmitters), including serotonin and adrenaline. Upon receiving this signal, stress hormones are released which particularly affect key areas of the brain for memory and regulating emotions. Repeated stress changes how well these systems are able to control the stress response.

Research suggests a biochemical link between stress and mental illness. Recent studies have shown that long-term stress can change the structure of the brain, especially in areas supporting learning and memory. It can affect both nerve cells (grey matter) and the connections between them (white matter). It is possible that these changes along with other factors can increase the likelihood of developing mental illness. About 30% of people with depression have increased inflammatory activity in the body. Researchers are also undertaking clinical trials to find out if anti-inflammatory drugs might be able to help people with this kind of depression. Increased levels of inflammation in the body over longer period of time is linked with life threatening physical health conditions and auto-immune disorders such as fibromyalgia, arthritis and multiple sclerosis.

The link between stress and physical health

Walter Cannon first confirmed the stress response system in the late 1920's. He called it 'fight or flight'. His observations and research proved that certain stressors such as lack of oxygen, extreme cold and emotional incidents, all lead to the release of stress hormones epinephrine and norepinephrine from the adrenal glands. Cannon discovered that the body's response to the release of epinephrine or the adrenaline rush is to increase the body's heart rate and breathing rate, dull pain, release sugar and fat and to bring blood away from digestion to the skeletal muscles. This highly complex physical response to our circumstances was originally designed to enable us to survive in life or death situations in times past to hunt well and to enable sharper focus and higher energy levels and muscular power. This provided much quicker thinking and movement for the short amount of time that the perceived 'risk' lasted.

Historically, the release of stress hormones would therefore be limited to short periods of minutes or hours or a few days at most in times of war. The body's stress response was only ever intended to last for short periods. Our bodies are not designed to withstand longer term, chronic effects of an increased heart rate and breathing pattern, dulled pain response, prolonged release of higher levels of sugar and fat or redistribution of blood from digestion to the skeletal muscles. When we live with long terms or chronic stress, we force our bodies to endure this unnatural state for periods that it was never built to withstand. Just like driving your car in the wrong gear for days on end, eventually something is going to give…

Conversely, when we remove the stressors from our lives and induce the body to stop releasing stress hormones from the adrenal glands, the body moves into the opposite state known as 'rest and digest'. During this state of reduced stress, the body's heart rate and breathing rate decrease, normal pain response is restored, sugar and fat is no longer released into the bloodstream and blood returns to the digestive system rather than being diverted to the skeletal muscles.

The importance of gut health is widely underestimated in society. It is a medical fact that 80% of our immune system lives in the gut. For as long as we remain in a state of stress, the normal blood flow to our gut, which is required for normal immune function, is disturbed. As blood flow is diverted away from the gut to our skeletal muscles to enable greater power and speed required for fight / flight, our digestive system becomes a lower priority. The digestive system is prepared for short periods of inadequate functioning but not for prolonged periods. Without an effective and fully functioning digestive system, we cannot have an effective and fully functioning immune system. This is a logical and obvious outcome of requiring 80% of the immune system to function at a disturbed level over a long period of time. We often pass off the poorer health that we suffer during times of stress as being 'run down'. The truth is that this is our immune system sending a clear message that it is not coping with the current set up and that something needs to change. Those coughs and colds and general lethargy are our body's way of telling us that it's time to drive using the proper gear. Failure to do so can only lead to more chronic issues which become more difficult to resolve and which sometimes become completely incurable.

Physical health – chronic conditions

Chronic (or long term) stress has a significant effect on the immune system that ultimately manifests as illness. It raises the body's levels of a chemical called catecholamine and reduces the number of active T cells levels (the cells that kill viruses and infections and so on). This has the effect of suppressing the natural processes of the immune system which in turn raises the risk of viral infection. During the stress response, the immune system is often 'artificially' activated or boosted by the body as it works hard to keep us safe. But chronic stress and prolonged 'artificial' activation of the immune system is not sustainable and can negatively affect how the brain functions.

Stress also leads to:

- The release of histamine which can trigger severe lung tightness in asthmatics.

- An increased risk for diabetes, especially in anyone who is overweight, since psychological stress alters insulin needs.
- Changes to the acid concentration in the stomach which can lead to peptic ulcers, stress ulcers or ulcerative colitis.
- Plaque build-up in the arteries (atherosclerosis), especially if combined with a high-fat diet and sedentary living.
- Psychiatric illness including neuroses, depression and schizophrenia.[1]

Researchers continue to work to better understand the cause-and-effect relationship between changes to the immune system and the development of cancer. Studies have found a link between stress, tumour development and suppression of those natural killer T-cells which are actively involved in preventing the spread of cancer and destroying small metastases (cancer cells) in the body[2]. This is an area of significant medical interest and developing knowledge. It logically follows that if the body is stressed and operating with a reduced amount of T cells (that are designed to help prevent the spread of cancer and to destroy cancerous cells), the risk of cancer becomes higher as a result.

---

[1] Life Event, Stress and Illness: Mohd. Razali Salleh Malaysian Journal of Medical Science
https://www.ncbi.nlm.nih.gov/pmc/articles/PMC3341916/

[2] Impact of stress on cancer metastasis : Myrthala Moreno-Smith, Susan K Lutgendorf and Anil K Sood Future Oncol 2010
https://www.ncbi.nlm.nih.gov/pmc/articles/PMC3037818/

Positive uses for manageable stress:

It is important to remember that not all stress is bad for the body or mind. Short term stress can have very positive effects. Stress at school or work or when competing may prompt motivation or drive, enabling us to achieve something worthwhile and help to develop new skills. Even the most stressful situations such as surviving cancer can have a positive effect on people's lives. Some cancer patients in remission emerge with a newfound spirituality or stronger self-esteem or empowerment because of the stress that they have endured and then triumphed. A personal battle with long-term health problems can be very difficult and stressful; however, some individuals start to develop a new sense of self-worth and new dreams and desires because of it. When someone survives an illness or life-threatening situation, they become more likely to truly live every day, to be thankful to be alive and to take better care of themselves and their environment.

When the body tolerates stress and uses it to overcome lethargy or to enhance performance, the stress is positive, healthy and challenging. Hans Selye, one of the pioneers of the modern study of stress, termed this 'eustress'. Stress is positive when it forces us to adapt and thus to increase the resilience of our adaptation mechanisms. It warns us that we are not coping well and that a lifestyle change is required if we are to maintain optimal health. This action-enhancing stress gives the athlete the competitive edge and the public speaker the enthusiasm to project optimally. We can use the physical changes in the body including increases in heart rate and breathing and increased tension in the muscles and improved short-term memory to our advantage. Stress is only negative when it exceeds our ability to cope, fatigues body systems and causes behavioural or physical problems. This harmful stress is called 'distress'. Distress produces overreaction, confusion, poor concentration and performance anxiety and it usually results in subpar performance. It is essential to listen to the body's warnings that we are under distress (or negative stress) and to make changes if we are to avoid the health issues which can flow from prolonged periods in this state.

By becoming aware of what specifically is causing us negative stress as individuals we can learn new strategies to reduce it and to better manage its impact upon our health and those around us.

Stress in the workplace:

The Mental Health Foundation in the UK has identified a clear need to effect changes in stress levels and stress management at a societal level. This includes ensuring that employers treat stress and mental health problems as seriously as physical safety. They suggest wellbeing days should be provided to public sector workers as part of reducing the pressure on those who work hardest to look after us. Recommendations have been made to the UK Government which included the need for further exploration of how the experience of stress can be reduced at the community and societal level. Employers are now required to address the issue of stress in the workplace as an epidemic and are obliged to help reduce it.

Stress impacts all of us differently. To some, it can feel like a mountain which is simply too big to climb or to others, its impact is not even recognised until it begins to be properly acknowledged and addressed. Whatever the impact, making change has to begin somewhere. If we can identify the stressors in our lives, we can begin to address them in a healthy and balanced way where results can be sustained. Finding new ways of coping with stress and increasing resilience can be fun and if they are enjoyable, will be more likely to endure.

Action:

1. **Acknowledge Stress:** Make a list of times when you feel stress levels increase. Notice where you are, who is around you, what is making you feel anxious, what are your fears? Are there any memories in your mind of things that have happened in your past? Notice how you feel in your body, too. Consider the impact that stress has upon you. Does it affect your sleep or ability to think clearly? Does it make you feel physically unwell? Do you suffer from any other medical condition that may be associated, for example stomach or bowel issues or joint pain or swelling, which may be connected to issues in the immune system? Is it affecting your relationships with your family or friends, either because you cannot find time to nurture those relationships or because you are short tempered? Write these things down and reflect upon how you can make changes to minimise your exposure to the environment that you find stressful.

2. **Take control of stress levels:** Make a choice to live in a different way and reduce the pressure that you are bringing

to your mind, body and soul. There are so many ways to start. Choose one that feels manageable and commit to it. Make it a habit. Perhaps a regular bedtime or meditation, perhaps restrictions on your drinking or committing to exercise three or four times per week. Then, once you have formed that habit, add another change and so on…Eventually, the upwards cycle of self-care will kick in and you will never want to go back. Let go of the stress that does not serve you well any longer and prioritise yourself and your own wellbeing above all and watch the positive changes flow…

Mantras for Stress Reduction:

- I am in charge of my stress response.
- In every moment, peace is a choice and I am peaceful.
- I notice and release / reduce stress.
- I let go of all that does not serve me.

Chapter 3
The Importance of Making Space

We have all experienced the feeling of overwhelm that comes with an over cluttered home or workspace at one time or another. We resolve to reorganise or throw things away that we no longer need, that are taking up valuable space and generally feel much better having cleared it out. In doing so, we also may come across little treasures that we had forgotten about or thought lost, buried under the rubbish. By de-cluttering we refresh our space and are left feeling rejuvenated and much more in control and organised. Just as this is true for our physical environment, it is also equally true of our bodies and minds. An internal and emotional spring clean is just as vital as de-cluttering our physical space.

Sometimes, life can feel like it is too much to manage well. Our schedules may be over committing us, leaving us no time to recharge or to have any fun. Worse still, a hectic and overly committed lifestyle leaves no time to choose how we spend our time in the moment. We are never free to wake up and reflect upon how we are feeling on any given day and respond by doing what our body or mind tells us it needs. How many times do we think 'I could really do with staying at home and resting today but I can't because I have to…' or 'I really need to go for a run to clear my head but I can't…' or 'I really wish I could spend the day with x today but I can't because I've already arranged…' The luxury of giving time to ourselves in response to our immediate needs is much more rare than it should be if we are truly practicing self-care.

Sometimes, we use our busy schedules as an excuse to avoid the tasks of self-care that we should really be practicing. We know that we should exercise but can't be bothered; we know that we should make time for that difficult conversation with a family member but we avoid it anyway. We excuse ourselves with our busy schedule but, in fact, we know that it is a convenient excuse for avoiding tasks which we will find difficult or emotional or which may lead to an outcome that we do not want. The trouble with leaving necessary tasks undone is that they don't usually go away on their own. Just as washing machines don't load and unload the laundry themselves, neither will the emotional laundry room clean the mind without some assistance. Action is required and if it is not taken, the dirty laundry remains and builds and clutters and takes up valuable space that could be being used for more positive things.

De-cluttering the home:

The key message in 'The life changing magic of tidying up' by Marie Kondo[3] is that tidying ought to be the act of restoring balance among people, their possessions and the

---

[3] The Life Changing Magic of Tidying Up by Maria Kondo

house they live in. In her beautiful book, Marie Kondo recommends that de-cluttering should begin with discarding anything that is no longer required or enjoyed. Once the space has been created, the thorough re-organisation can begin, completely and in one go. Kondo notes that the work involved in tidying up can be broadly divided into two kinds: deciding whether or not to dispose of something and if an item is to be kept, deciding where to put it. She recommends keeping only those things that inspire joy. She notes that by dramatically reducing the volume of things we own, we will experience a new exhilaration and gain confidence in our lives.

Looked at in this way, the physical act of tidying becomes simple. For each item of clutter, we have to answer only three questions: 1) Do I want to keep it? If so, 2) Does it bring me joy? If the answers to questions 1 and 2 are both yes (and only then), we keep it and move to question 3, which is 'Where should I put it?' (Where does it belong?) It may be that we cannot find a place for it and so in searching for its correct place, the item is discarded. We may recognise its lack of importance or meaning to us and therefore, it becomes less necessary to take up valuable space. In applying this method, we create an environment where we are surrounded only by things that bring positivity into our lives. We get rid of anything that sparks a negative memory or message and we are once again able to see and enjoy the little treasures once lost under the clutter. By following this process, we will eventually live in an environment that is entirely of our creation, not only by what is in it but by how it is ordered too. We will truly own the space that surrounds us, feel positive and relaxed being within it and will be better able and more motivated to take care of it.

Sounds very appealing, doesn't it? Who wouldn't want to be surrounded by that environment? Answer: Only those who choose not to change! Some people are not ready to de-clutter. For some, the task seems completely overwhelming. When we are ready to clear out, we will find the motivation and the time and energy required to do so. The same can be said for de-cluttering the body and mind.

De-cluttering the mind:

The sound and logical principles, that underpin Marie Kondo's theory of tidying up our environment, also apply to the clearing out of the mind. To achieve an optimum environment for mental and physical health to thrive, we must not hold on to worries which belong in our past and we must not worry about anything which has not yet happened. It is essential to focus on the 'now' and to live more mindfully with our concentration and focus fully applied to our lives in the present moment. The human body and mind is a great feat of engineering, fully equipped to declutter and keep only what it needs. Physically and mentally the body is not designed to hold onto things that it does not need and which are not good for it. The body and mind are adept at making space. However, the way that we live in our modern age sometimes prevents our well-oiled machines from working as they should. Our heightened stress levels mean that we hold onto experiences and negative feelings by worrying. Our processed diet causes us to ingest substances that the body cannot cleanse away easily, such as gluten, chemicals or parasites. These are the things that our body and mind do not need. Holding onto the rubbish prevents our minds and bodies from working as efficiently as they should. It also takes up valuable space that is needed for what should be there to work well and for new more positive things to take root.

We can actively tidy our minds using the same Kondo principles to achieve the same results. We can create an environment where we are surrounded only by thoughts and memories that bring positivity into our lives. We can rid ourselves of anything that sparks a negative memory or message so that we are once again able to see and enjoy the little treasures once lost under the clutter. We can choose to live in a mental health environment that is entirely of our creation, not only by what is in it but how it is ordered too. We own the space in our minds and by taking control of it, we feel positive and relaxed being within it and are better able and more motivated to take care of it.

The first step to being able to clear out the mind of the trash is to truly accept that we are in control of our thoughts rather than our thoughts being in control of us. We can no longer accept any suggestion that 'our minds are running away with us' or that we 'can't stop thinking about something'. Our thoughts are created by our own consciousness and we are our consciousness! We, therefore, create our own thoughts and it follows that we can also stop those thoughts or re-direct them if we want to. We can train our brains to behave differently. The key to changing negative thought patterns is a genuine desire to change our way of thinking and an acceptance that we have the power to do so. Some of us are entrenched in patterns of self-harm through over analysing, our conduct, words, behaviour, sometimes from years ago and with no prospect whatsoever of changing what happened. Rehearsing past events can appear to bring some odd kind of comfort when we are in that destructive thought pattern, our minds deceiving us into thinking that if we somehow re-work the situation in our minds, it will resolve the anxiety that we attach to it. This is not true. We cannot change the past and thinking about something bad that happened will continue to bring the same bad feelings and vibrations to us that we had when we first experienced it.

If this is true for you, think about why you are doing this to yourself. Why do you think you are not worthy of being rid of that bad experience? Who or what made you feel that way? What happened to you in your life that has made you feel that you don't deserve peace of mind or to feel good about yourself or to be happy? The truth is that each of us deserves to have peace of mind to feel good about ourselves and to be as happy as we can possibly be. To deliver that to ourselves, however, we have to choose to let go and be rid of the anxiety and pain and discomfort that holding on to this memory brings. Forgive yourself if you need to but if self-blame is in any way attached to this negative experience, ask yourself this: Were you doing the best that you could do at the time with the information that was available? If the answer is yes then you have nothing to forgive yourself for. Let yourself be at peace and let it go…If you made a poor choice than take comfort in the fact that the anxiety this poor behaviour or conduct has brought to you proves that you have learned from it. You will never make the same choice again. That is positive. That made the experience one worth having. Take the positive away from the negative experience. Separate the two. Keep the positive lesson but let the negative experience go…

Of course, there are some experiences that impact upon us in ways that are too fundamental to control. Trauma can affect our minds in far reaching and devastating ways. When this applies to us, we should seek professional help. Trauma is our body's response to what has happened to it and it can be manipulated into a more positive frame. There is no shame in asking for help with cleaning up our mental health. We cannot change our experiences but we can manage our responses to it in a healthy way. We must not allow ourselves to become a victim, impacted negatively by experiences indefinitely. Seeking help from professionals can help to reframe the experience to enable us to feel safe, secure and in control again. A GP, a friend or family member, Cruse, Mind or the Samaritans are all fantastic places to start a journey back to positive mental health.

If you have identified something in your mind that doesn't serve you well any longer and that you want to get rid of then find a way to expel it. You wouldn't allow a person to stay in your home uninvited who made you feel badly about yourself and brought misery to you every day, so don't let gremlins live inside your mind and have the same effect. If you were unable to evict your unwanted lodger from your home by yourself, you would seek assistance to do so. The same applies to the emotional and psychological gremlins. Evict whatever doesn't bring you joy and make space for what does. A regular meditative or mindfulness practice is a good way to enable us to take control of those racing thoughts to become the master of our own minds rather than our minds determining what we focus on. The mind is not the enemy. By being more selective about what we carry in our minds, we create space to develop positive thinking patterns and to learn new patterns of mental, emotional and psychological behaviour.

So, what should we keep in our minds and what should we expel? Start by applying the same principles as we would to tidying up the home. Ask: Do I need it and does it bring me joy? If not, get rid of it. Whenever it pops into our mind, we notice it and choose to expel it from our mind in favour of a more positive thought or memory. Without any judgment, just let it float away. For this to work effectively, the answer to whether we need it to whether it brings us joy must be answered honestly. No excuses!

Finally, if we decide that we are going to keep the thought or memory in our minds, we need to decide where to put it. Where to order it. Is it something that will be allowed to float in and out of our minds or will we allocate a specific time each day or week to ponder upon it? The point is that we each take control of what will and will not be allowed to occupy the precious space inside of us. We fully accept that we each own our own thinking. The more we conduct this exercise, the easier it is to implement and the more quickly we will notice thoughts that are not serving us well. Starting a mindfulness or meditation habit or practice is so helpful in learning how to notice our thoughts floating in and out of our mind before they take hold and teaching us how to control them.

De-cluttering the body:

Maintaining a physical body that is clear of debris and toxicity is a crucial factor in maintaining good overall health and a sense of positive wellbeing. If we have spent years consuming poor quality 'fuel' it affects the efficiency of our gut. Our bodies become less proficient at absorbing what we do need from our food and expelling what we don't need. Toxins, parasites and other waste can build up to exacerbate the problem. Moreover, as 80% of the immune system lives in the gut, other aspects of our physical health may become affected too. Poor gut health can also manifest itself physcially but also as a feeling of sluggishness, tiredness, brain fog or a general lack of motivation. To address this problem, we need a gut clean-up. There are many ways to do it. Firstly, we have to de-clutter. This can be done by a salt water flush or similar, which literally flushes through the colon and rids the body of a multitude of waste residing there. A number of supplements exist to implement this process more slowly if drinking salted water does not appeal! Lots of juice detox's and fasting cleanses may have a similar effect. An array of parasitic cleanses, usually supplement based, are available to rid the body of any little nasties that may not be flushed away by other means.

Once we have de-cluttered and rid ourselves of the rubbish, we must reorder the environment. Make conscious decisions about what you intend to put into your body from then on. Choose well. It is entirely possible to eat well and enjoy it! As we cleanse our stomach of the enzymes that feed on junk food by starving them, they will not multiply. Instead, the enzymes that feed on nutritious food will become abundant, causing us to desire more healthy food and shun the less nutritious junk. Getting rid of sugar cravings will help shift the desire for sweet food, enabling more enjoyment of healthy and nutritious alternatives as we finally begin to taste it fully! Drink plenty of water to keep everything moving well through the gut area. Certain foods such as broccoli and dark leafy greens will help move food through the colon efficiently. It is also extremely beneficial to add fermented foods and additional fibre to your diet in some way. These contain probiotics and prebiotics, which help to maintain the gastro-intestinal system and keep it healthy.

Yoga is a fantastic way to de-clutter the body and mind. The fundamental principles of yoga are proper exercise (Asanas), proper breathing (Pranayama), proper relaxation (i.e., Savasana), proper diet, positive thinking and meditation. Yoga asana requires us to place the body under a manageable amount of physical stress which switches on our sympathetic nervous system (increases our heart rate and energy flow around the body). At the same time, we consciously slow our breathing and take control of our thoughts, therefore, reducing the heart rate and consciously switching on the parasympathetic nervous system, overriding the stress. This process trains our bodies and minds to be able to maintain control, focus and a calm disposition under stress and indeed in everyday situations. The physical benefits to the body are extraordinary as regular practice enables the loosening of tight areas and creates a feeling of easier movement, releasing chonic 'somatic' stress that has become stuck in the body over time. Strength is improved also but without the discomfort of the lactic acid build-up of a traditional weights or cardio programme. In lengthening and stretching muscles and improving muscular-skeletal movement we release tension and anxiety, creating space and comfort in the body as well as training the mind to maintain composure under pressure.

Owning our environment:

Tidying up our environment, whichever environment it may be, gives us a feeling of control and ownership, which in turn promotes happiness and encourages a practice of good maintenance. Everything feels fresh, clean, manageable and more joyous. We are able to see and take pleasure from the lost treasures. We are less willing to accept clutter back in. We start to live differently. We begin to notice the importance of making choices about what and who we surround ourselves with, including people and interactions as well as belongings. Making space is fundamental to letting the parts of us breath that had previously been stifled. It is essential to make space to let new things in, which are always better suited to us than something meaningless that we picked up mindlessly ten years ago! It is easier to breath in an open space. It is easier to respond to events rather than to react. Let the light back into the dark corners by clearing out the clutter and starting afresh. Make space for all the wonder of life that is still to come…Make space for the things that are especially chosen by you, for you.

MANTRA for Making Space: I let go of all that does not serve me.

Reflection: Make a list of three things that are special to you with space underneath each one to write more.

Reflect upon each object and why it has made the list! Where did it come from? Who bought it for you? Does it have monetary value? Now beside each item make a list of the emotions that you attach to each belonging. How does it make you feel to look at it or see it? Does it remind you of a happy time or a person? Try to identify what it triggers in you that is positive.

Now think about other things, either belongings or experiences that make you feel this way. Had you placed value on those things before? Can you make more time and space to do more of the things that bring you the positive feeling? Is there a way that you can use your favourite belongings more to bring you greater happiness, perhaps placing them in view or using them more regularly?

Now make a list of three items in your house that have a negative impact upon you and why. Why do you keep this item? Why do you keep it if it brings bad feeling? Can you do without it? If not, is there a way to change the way you view it to make it less negative in your mind?

Chapter 4
Setting Your Satnav

It is often difficult to identify what we want to change about our lives, especially if faced with trying to unpick years of not taking proper care of ourselves. It may be that one or two areas immediately shout out for assistance but it is likely that there are more areas that could do with increased awareness than we might expect. Some of us come to a self-improvement journey with a complete sense of overwhelm, being unable to see the wood for the trees. This is often accompanied by a sense of hopelessness which is difficult to live with and which reaches into every area of life. Whatever brings us to the realisation that it is time to make improvements and wherever we ultimately end up, we must find a place to begin. A useful place to start is to quantify our sense of self-worth.

A good way to do this is to write a list of ten things that you appreciate and value in the world. Take time to find a pen and scribble on the inside cover of the book if you have to. When you have written the list, number everything on it in the order that it was written. If you intend to undertake this exercise then do not read on until you have completed it…

Now you have written a list and numbered the items on it, look for yourself. Are you on your own list? So many of us forget how wonderful we actually are as human beings. Some of us are unable to recognise the value that we bring to the world or to others. Most of us find it difficult to acknowledge out loud that we are a person to be proud of.

The fundamental core of wellbeing requires us to place value on ourselves. Wellness requires time and commitment to achieve. The process will sometimes be tough and we will sometimes have to motivate ourselves do things that are good for us but which we don't actually want to do in that moment. We have to find discipline to make our goals a reality. We have to commit to our success. The benefits will become obvious within a very short space of time and the dedication to self will be worth the effort. Anything is possible over time if we are committed to it. In our busy modern lives, the road to comfort, peace, health and happiness requires us to prioritise ourselves over and above the needs of others at times, which may feel like a challenge if we are used to deferring our needs to those of others. We may also need to carve out precious time to use just for ourselves. This can be tough if we are balancing other competing demands on our time, especially of loved ones.

It can sometimes be challenging to make regular space, even for something that we really think is really important; something that we already place value upon. It is challenging but we manage it because we prioritise that objective that we value. Conversely, we are much less likely to achieve a goal which is based in progressing something we do not value. So it is essential to ensure that we are placing ourselves in the 'valued' category if we want to succeed in making lasting change. We have to understand that there is value in us as individuals and in our own lives. We have to feel worthy of receiving our own time, effort, change, progress and success.

Early life experiences often shape the way that we feel about ourselves. We are born perfect and hopefully are treated as such by those who care for us. As we grow, we start to become conditioned by our environment and by our family and friends. We cannot help but be impacted negatively sometimes and conditioned in ways that don't suit us, even by the most well-meaning caregivers and teachers. We accept all that is told to us as being true. As a child, we have no basis upon which to think it would not be so or would not be in our best interests. From time to time we may experience something that makes us feel like the stupid one in class, the less important sibling, the less attractive one in the friendship group, the overweight one, the skinny one, the brainy one, the pretty one. As a child, we have no reason or means by which to challenge those labels. If they are reinforced often enough, we become accepting of those labels and begin to live by them. We live and behave as if we are the stupid one or the less important one. That label is likely to become what we perceive ourselves to be. In living by these false 'truths', we start to create our own destiny in line with a label that we don't like and which, if we dig a little deeper, was never actually justified at all.

We may also have had an experience which made us feel worthless or not deserving of good things. This can happen at any age but the consequences may resonate throughout our whole life if we do not make peace with it. If left unchecked, this trauma response may act as a blockage to progress and change and could require professional psychological input to resolve, especially if it has led to long standing behavioural changes.

As we progress through life, we collect these labels and different perspectives about our identity. We also become more automated and less conscious about our existence. We do more because we think we should or because that's 'what I do' or what is expected of us and less through conscious decision making. As we operate in this automated way, facing all of the pressures of modern society, we employ all of our most primitive 'reptilian' tendencies (our 'limbic system') to survive.

As we strive to succeed and to keep up with the relentless pace of modern living, it becomes increasingly difficult to identify with who we truly are. Our authenticity gets lost. When we are under stress or feel threatened in some way, the limbic system is fully engaged. Our more primitive reptilian tendencies and instinct kicks in and drives us to be focussed on survival and control. Our pre frontal cortex, the area of our brains which helps us to be more relaxed and more connected with our emotions, becomes less active. Unfortunately, as we push ourselves forward, hoping to move through the stress and eventually escape it, we do so unconsciously and with our limbic system in the driving seat. This means that the decisions we take in those stressful moments are focussed on survival and success rather than happiness and fulfilment. We are not striving for balance and peace but instead are aggressively in pursuit of completely the opposite. We are less consciously aware and often in something of a trance, not connected with our real self. It is a natural and biological reaction borne of necessity in times past. Today, in our world of self-made pressure, it is no longer necessary to manage our lives in this way. To do so has become a habit, however, and great self-awareness and determination is required to be more conscious of what is driving us as we push for change and self-improvement.

As we move through our wellbeing experience towards a greater sense of fulfilment and balance, it is important to become more aware of the patterns that navigate us through life. That awareness allows us to consciously decide whether we want to continue to live in those patterns. It is helpful to ensure that as often as possible, our clear thinking, unbiased true self is in the driving seat so that we can make decisions consciously rather than through habit. Our decision making will be more informed, reliable and gratifying. Importantly, the outcomes will be better for us if we make life decisions when connected with our head and with our heart together and in a more relaxed state.

When we are fully engaged in awareness and are focussed on what is happening 'now', we are not distracted by our environment, patterning, habits or by others. We are fully connected with ourselves. We are out of the trance that we have become so used to operating within. The more time we spend in this state of awareness with our true and fully connected selves in the driving seat, the better equipped we are to notice when we are simply reacting and not truly responding to our life experiences in a conscious way. The more we notice this in ourselves, the easier it becomes to see it in others. We become more meaningfully connected to those around us and also more tolerant. It becomes easier to see when others are reacting and not meaningfully responding to what is happening around them. In turn, we are able to take negative behaviours less personally and to understand that often the goodness in others is eclipsed by their own patterning, conditioning, stress or other environmental factors. Life becomes much more meaningful, simply because we can finally see it! And once we can see it, we are more easily able to decide the path that we want to take and the environment that we want to create for ourselves.

Is it time to create new labels? Perhaps it is time to make different decisions about what you want to be. What do you want to be? Making a list of the things that we want to change about ourselves is often recommended by self-help books eager to direct those individuals who are longing for change. This can be a very useful tool but there are two very important notes of caution to offer to this type of work:

- Firstly, any changes that we make to ourselves should always be seen positively as personal growth rather than getting rid of anything 'bad,' to avoid viewing ourselves through a negative lens. Self-acceptance is key both in terms of our current behaviour and also how we have behaved in the past. Radical or complete self acceptance enables us to move on in a sustainable and peaceful way. It is easier to accept our past negative or harmful behaviours and indeed becomes possible to change them for good if we can understand what was driving that mind-set and decision making. We may not like the person that we once were but the truth of our behaviours has to be acknowledged and understood to be accepted and, therefore, to be adapted in a meaningful and sustainable way. Self forgiveness and being kind to ourselves provides the most stable platform to build upon.

What we think we want to achieve from a wellbeing initiative at the outset is rarely what we actually need, nor is it usually aligned with the outcome that we will ultimately be content with further down the line. Any list that we make about ourselves will always be a working document to be regularly reviewed and modified. As we develop greater self-esteem, self-awareness and confidence, all of which are an inevitable consequence of self-development and personal growth, we will surely come to accept that some of what is on our original list is not important or desirable after all. New objectives will be added to the list, too as fresh possibilities open up and as priorities change.

- Secondly, it is essential that if we make a list of the parts of us that we want to be different, we also make a list of the parts of us that are good, valuable and precious and which we want to retain. These lists are a reflection of our sense of self-worth. In utilising the positive list as a working document and adding to it as we grow, we reinforce the good progress that we are making. There may also be items on this list that we decide are better placed on the list of things we want to change and that's OK too! As we grow and become more satisfied with ourselves and with the balance that we have created, this second list will be overflowing with positive things that we can identify about ourselves. This provides greater motivation to keep working on self-improvement and towards greater contentment and balance.

It is contrary to human nature to allow things to flow without any sense of control or direction. Modern life has taught us to grasp for things that may not be beneficial, to value superficial things. Consumerism encourages the need for unecessary 'stuff.' We are in the habit of handing over our personal power and outsourcing our wellbeing. In a process of personal growth, however, the best results tend to materialise from a state of flow and letting go of the need to control everything. Being open minded to whatever may happen provides the best environment for growth and personal development. Being prepared to try new things and being open to new ideas will broaden the spectrum of what is possible and make new horizons brighter and more likely to bring positive change. This is not easy as control brings predictability and a feeling of safety, making it hard to relinquish, but the effort is worth the reward.

So, in setting your sat nav for your journey of personal growth and development, do have some ideas about what you would like to change and what you want to keep. Have in mind though that the more open we keep the intended destination and the more agreeable we are to exploring alternative and unexpected routes, the more likely it is that we will organically flourish and grow towards the person that we actually are. Narrowing objectives at the outset makes it much more likely that any growth will be dictated by the life conditioning and more closed mind-set that currently drives decision making, all of which is best avoided on the path to genuine wellbeing and life balance.

MANTRA for personal growth: I am open to experience all that life has to offer me. I am open to understanding my higher purpose.

Reflection:

Think how easily you accept a compliment. Do you dispute kind things that are said to you or do you gratefully accept the praise with a 'thank you'? Think of a compliment that you have had recently. Write it down here:

Do you agree with what was said? If not, why not?
Write down five things that you really like about yourself?

Write down five things that are unique or special about you?

Have you identified these positive traits because you like them about yourself or because you think that they are valued by others?
These exercises are great ways of really drilling down on how we really feel about ourselves and whether we place value on ourselves, only through how we are perceived by others.

Write down five things that others like about you.

Underline the ones that you agree with. How important are the things that are not underlined? Do you feel compelled to keep those parts of you just because others think you should? If so, this would be a really helpful area of work to undertake.

The next time you receive a compliment, smile and say thank you. Then add the compliment to your list of things you like about yourself. Refer to it whenever you are feeling low to remind yourself of all of the things that are positive about you.

Chapter 5
The Mind, Body and Spirit as One Moving Part

Our system of modern medicine has evolved in the most peculiar way. Our initial point of call for non-emergency ailments is our GP who considers our complaint from a general perspective. The GP takes their best educated assessment as to which discipline of secondary medicine could help us investigate our issue further and so we wait to discuss diagnosis, prognosis and treatment with an 'expert' in the relevant field. Only very infrequently, though will we be referred to more than one field of secondary care at any one time. So, we await our consultant or investigative appointments with hope and expectation. In the event that investigations prove fruitless, a second referral to an alternative discipline will be made and so the process continues.

The system works on the principle that each area of the body and mind is distinct and operates separately from one another. So, for example, an issue with brain fog and memory issues would be referred to neurology for further investigation, most likely MRI scanning and blood tests. It is rare that a GP would ask about diet, childhood or sleep patterns during such a consultation. It is even more unlikely that a GP would refer such matters to endocrinology for hormone investigation or thyroid function or to a nutritionist or psychologist to analyse whether there was any link between the presenting symptoms and gut function, toxicity, adrenal failure or stress.

It is now common practice in some disciplines, particularly in oncology, to make use of multidisciplinary teams in care and treatment planning. This enables the oncologist, radiographer and specialist discipline of the biological system impacted by the cancer to work alongside the pathologist, psychologist, haematologist, community care or occupational health or physiotherapy teams. The patient receives a more rounded and holistic approach to their physical care, recognising the need to treat a number of different elements of the illness with which the patient has been diagnosed as well as symptomatic presentation. This can only be of benefit. What the current general healthcare model continues to miss is the biological link between different parts of the body and the link between our psychological, endocrine, immune and neurological systems and indeed the unavoidable fact that any discord in one part of the body will inevitably increase the risk of issues elsewhere.

During the nineteenth century, the microbiologist, Louis Pasteur (of pasteurisation fame!), and the physiologist, Claude Barnard, entered into lengthy theoretical debate about what caused some people to become very sick from a virus whilst the same virus had a barely noticeable impact upon others. They disagreed as to whether it was the strength of a virus (Pasteur) or the vulnerability of the host body (Barnard) that dictated the impact of illness. Pasteur continued to maintain that the strength of the virus was the sole determining factor until his death bed when he conceded that Barnard was correct in attributing the outcome to the vulnerability of the sick individual. Western medicine now generally accepts that the vulnerability of the immune system affects how we may react to any given illness. What remains more of a mystery, however, even to this day is what makes one host body vulnerable to illness whilst another's immune system deals swiftly with an identical threat.

Science has demonstrated a link between certain environmental factors and illness such as: smoking and lung cancer or an unhealthy lifestyle and heart failure. That same science still cannot explain why two individuals who smoke in equal measure will not both develop cancer, however, why some people can live to a ripe old age despite drinking, eating badly and rarely exercising. Our bodies are designed to withstand significant illness and to heal themselves in remarkable ways. The cell mutation that has the potential to cause cancer is happening constantly in our bodies, whether through old age or environmental factors such as drinking or smoking and is usually recognised by the cell itself. Illness does not usually result from mutation because of the biological systems already in place to stop that mutated cell from multiplying or by beginning a process known as 'programmed cell death' (apoptosis), which the body uses to get rid of unneeded cells. If that process fails then our immune system is usually ready to kill off any cells which do not appear to be 'normal' and so we remain healthy.

What happens though if our cells do not recognise that those cells are mutated and so continue to grow? What makes that process fail? What if our immune system is compromised in some way and cannot manage its task of ridding the body of mutated cells? At this point, simplistically, the mutated cells multiply, a tumour is formed and so the cancer begins…

Research tells us that a healthy lifestyle is important to avoid illness and disease and that is no longer a controversial proposition. Examples of how we can reduce our cancer risk, for example, most usually include reducing our alcohol consumption and stopping smoking, reducing sun exposure, eating more healthily and engaging in exercise! This advice is of course based fimly in common sense because in living well (physically) we are reducing our intake of and exposure to toxins, therefore reducing the risk of cell mutation through environmental factors in the first place. These environmental chemicals and toxins have been identified by researchers as creating a 'cancer stimulating' environment. As we strive to reduce our risk of becoming unwell, we may begin to question the impact upon our bodies of the chemicals that are contained within the food that we eat (pesticides, fertilisers, glyphosate, fluoride or lead and other heavy metals in our water supply); in the soap or detergents that we use to wash our bodies and our clothes which sit next to our skin all day; in the chemicals that we use to clean our homes and work spaces which we ingest and breathe; in the micro-plastics in our food chain due to pollution or by microwaving with cling film or through the use of plastic food containers or water bottles or coffee cups.

These small ways in which we absorb foreign substances into our bodies accumulate over time. Our bodies are not biologically equipped to cope with them. Basic common sense dictates that this must have an impact upon the environment we create for our cells as they go about their business of dividing and multiplying, recreating our complex genetic code as they do so. As an example of the way these small toxins can build up in our bodies, the World Wildlife Fund International concluded in an independentstudy that we could each be ingesting the equivalent of a credit card of plastic every week! Over the average lifetime, that's more plastic than it takes to make two family sized wheelie bins. Biologically, how can our bodies even begin to process that? Nano plastic particles are so small that they are able to flow through our bodies in our blood and cross the blood brain barrier and in to the brain itself.

So, we know that a physically healthy lifestyle is important and that it is helpful to reduce toxicity to improve our health prospects but physical lifestyle changes alone cannot ensure overall wellbeing or even a level of physical health that is sufficient to prevent disease. To have the best chance of an optimal immune system, for example, we have to look more deeply at the way the body works and examine the physical, psychological, emotional and environmental factors that affect the performance of our immunology.

The field of neuro-psycho-immunoendocrinology is a developing field of research that explores the link between a brain (neuro), psychology (psycho), immune system (immuno) and endocrine or hormone systems (endocrinology). It is an important emerging scientific field of research that improves our understanding of the mind-body connection, studying the links between psychological processes and the nervous, endocrine and immune systems of the physical body. Dr Robert Ader, a distinguished University Professor at the University of Rochester School of Medicine and Dentistry, describes the life balance of the individual [homeostasis] as "an integrated process involving interactions among behaviour and the nervous, endocrine, and immune systems".[4]

In short, Western science is gradually coming to accept what the Eastern philosophies have understood for years, namely that the mind and body are one integrated moving part. As such, it is not possible for damage or failure of one part of our machine to exist in isolation. It will always have an impact upon something else. We see this physically when we hurt our knee and are not surprised when our back begins to ache also, or our hip starts to play up. We explain this as a consequence of our bodies being forced to function differently to accommodate the failure of the knee. We may readily accept that problems elsewhere are as a result of us walking or distributing our weight differently. We are generally accepting of the impact that our original injury or malfunction will have on other parts of the body. In some ways, Western society is also accepting of the suggestion that psychological issues can impact upon our physical bodies. The widely accepted link between acute stress and heart problems is an obvious example. We also know that we feel psychological responses physically – we feel nerves or excitement in our stomachs and not in our heads; fear can make us sick. Why then does Western medicine find it a challenge to accept that an issue with our physical body, gut health, our hormones or a psychological response may cause a problem within our immune system or vice versa?

---

[4] On the development of psychoneuroimmunology - Robert Ader - published in 'Science Direct' 2000
https://www.sciencedirect.com/science/article/abs/pii/S0014299900005501

The Science:

The immune system, the major process of the body's self-defence, is extremely complex involving the central nervous and endocrine systems. There is growing evidence for the suggestion that endocrine system (the various glands which produces and release hormones into the body and the hypothalamus in our brain which controls that process) directly influence the development and function of the immune system. Clinical observations suggest that many disorders of the blood, cancer and immune system disfunction are associated with changes to the body's natural ability to balance hormones. The close relationship and interplay between the central nervous system and hormone system may well be of importance for the body's defence against infectious and cancerous diseases, too.

Studies in Western medicine are beginning to establish a link between a healthy gut micro-biome (the genetic material of all the microbes – bacteria, fungi, protozoa and viruses that live on and inside the human gut) and illness. A study in 2017 showed for the first time that chronic (long term) inflammation was caused by gut bacteria. This low-grade chronic inflammation is linked to life-limiting conditions such as stroke, dementia and heart disease. The research brought with it the hope of a potentially simple strategy to contribute to healthy ageing, as the composition of bacteria in the gut is, at least in part, controlled by diet. The results suggested that an imbalance of the composition in the gut may be the cause of inflammation. An overgrowth of bad bacteria can make the lining of the gut become more permeable, allowing toxins to enter the bloodstream where they can travel around the body with various negative effects and serious health implications[5]. Several disorders such as inflammatory bowel disease, obesity, diabetes, cancer, anxiety and autism have been significantly linked to poor gut function.

Signals run from the gut to other parts of our bodies via neurons, hormones and the immune system through pathways called 'axis'. The most studied axis so far is the connection between gut and brain. It is documented and well-known among health professionals that patients suffering from inflammatory bowel diseases often also suffer from depression. Signals between the gut and brain travel through the axis known as the 'Vagus nerve'. Astonishingly, 80–90% of fibres carry messages from gut to brain and only 10–20% carry messages from brain to gut. The gut is able to alter the brain chemistry through neurons and through the messengers of the immune system called 'cytokines.' The efficient functioning of all of this depends upon the state of the gut, which is impacted by all sorts of internal and external factors. Stress is a good example: Stress changes the composition of the gut micro-biome which in turn results in a depleted immune response.

Another important link to the gut in the body is the gut-liver axis, which has been studied widely in liver research, as

---

[5] Floris Fransen, Adriaan A. van Beek, Theo Borghuis, Sahar El Aidy, Floor Hugenholtz, Christa van der Gaast – de Jongh, Huub F. J. Savelkoul, Marien I. De Jonge, Mark V. Boekschoten, Hauke Smidt, Marijke M. Faas, Paul de Vos. Aged Gut Microbiota Contributes to Systemical Inflammaging after Transfer to Germ-Free Mice. Frontiers in Immunology, 2017;
8 DOI: 10.3389/fimmu.2017.01385

70% of the blood flow to the liver directly flows from the gut and so may impact the risk of fatty liver disease. The gut-lung axis has been widely studied in respiratory disease research, where gut health influences both asthma, COPD, pneumonia and even development of cancer. Scientists have also proposed a gut-kidney axis where the toxic products of a diseased kidney affect the gut function and this disturbance increases the number of toxins released into the body. It seems clear then that the function of our gut is linked to our overall health and the importance of creating and maintaining a healthy gut environment cannot be underestimated.

The impact of positive thinking on the physical body:

Emotional and psychological health has a huge impact upon our physical functioning too. Findings in a study led by Lisa Yanek, Assistant Professor of Medicine (M.P.H.)[6], showed that positivity made a highly significant difference to outcomes. Even in people with family history of coronary artery disease and who had the most environmental risk factors, positive people from the general population were 13% less likely than their negative counterparts to have a heart attack or other coronary event. 'Positivity' was assessed by measuring a person's cheerfulness, energy level, anxiety levels and satisfaction with health and overall life. Researchers also suspect that people who are more positive may be better protected against the inflammatory damage of

---

[6] Effect of Positive Well-Being on Incidence of Symptomatic Coronary Artery Disease Lisa R. Yanek, MPH, et al 2015
https://www.ncbi.nlm.nih.gov/pmc/articles/PMC3788860/

stress. It is thought that hope and positivity help people make better health and life decisions and focus more on long-term goals. Studies have also discovered that negative emotions can weaken immune response and that a positive attitude improves outcomes and life satisfaction across a spectrum of conditions including traumatic brain injury, stroke and brain tumours.

The impact of positivity on pain:

Researchers at Peking University discovered in 2019[7] that cancer patients experienced less chronic pain when they engaged in activities which showed kindness to others. Such acts of kindness, which release natural endorphins into the bloodstream, were shown to be more than twice as effective as a chemical pain killer. Experiments also showed that healthy subjects who had acted selflessly immediately before testing experienced less physical discomfort from needle jabs and electric shocks. These findings add to existing evidence that helping others can improve wellbeing by reducing stress and blood pressure as well as increasing longevity. Positive thinking and the benefits of community support are powerful tools in our wellness armoury.

There is a wealth of evidence to support the basic common sense suggestion that our bodies, minds and spirits are all completely enmeshed and co-dependent. One depends upon

---

[7] Altruistic behaviors relieve physical pain - Yilu Wang, Jianqiao Ge, Hanqi Zhang, Haixia Wang, and Xiaofei Xie - PNAS January 14, 2020 117 (2) 950-958; first published December 30, 2019 https://doi.org/10.1073/pnas.1911861117

the other for efficient functioning and so we cannot be in optimum physically health if we are struggling emotionally or psychologically and vice versa. Equally, we cannot expect to maintain optimum immune function if we are not eating well. No area can be ignored in the quest for living well. We have to think of ourselves as one moving part rather than a series of unrelated bits and pieces which just happen to be linked by the skin they exist within. By thinking about our health and wellbeing in a more holistic way, we are more likely to be able to identify the root cause of any threat to our wellbeing and health and even better to be able to prevent it from causing us harm.

MANTRA for connected living: My head is clear, my heart is open and my soul is purposeful.

Reflection:

Think about any short term or long term health issues that you suffer from. Consider how it might be improved by improving other areas of your life? Examples include better sleep, a little more exercise, relaxation techniques (such as mindfulness, meditation or yoga) or a cleaner diet. Can you give yourself slight advantages or improvements in a few different areas which will accumulate to result in a noticeable improvement to your health?

Action:

Identify one change that you will make and maintain every day for two weeks. Record the changes that you feel as a result, not just in that one area but in all areas: psychologically, physically, cognitively (in the brain such as clearer thinking or better memory) and in terms of energy, sleep hygiene and general health.

Chapter 6
Love

Love is at the heart of a balanced and healthy lifestyle. As human beings, we all need affection, connection, attachment and to give and receive acts of kindness to survive. This can be a positive feeling of loving kindness towards ourselves or feelings of affection received by other. We see this basic human need used against prisoners who are socially isolated as a means of punishment, to devastating effect. Healthy and optimally functioning individuals who are kept in isolation eventually suffer significant psychological as well as physical deterioration. We see the 'time out' exclusion from the family or peer group being used as a punishment for young children, and imprisonment as a punishment for criminal behaviour. Studies have shown that adults who are more socially connected are healthier and live longer than their more isolated peers. Researchers describe major findings in the study of social relationships and health, recording that relationships shape health outcomes throughout life and have a cumulative impact on health over time.

Community Resilience:

The importance of community on resilience and strength cannot be underestimated. A person's social network can have a significant impact on their health. One large scale, international study[8] showed that over seven years, those with adequate social relationships had a 50% greater survival rate from chronic disease compared to individuals with poor social relationships. Social networks (not to be confused with social media networks which do not quite have the same effect) have been shown to be predictors of mortality as powerful as common lifestyle and clinical risks such as moderate smoking, excessive alcohol consumption, obesity high cholesterol and blood pressure. Social support is particularly important in increasing resilience and promoting recovery from illness. A lack of social networks or support and chronic loneliness produce long-term damage to physiological health through raised stress hormone levels, poorer immune function and cardiovascular health. Loneliness also makes it harder to self-regulate behaviour and build willpower and resilience over time, leading to engagement in unhealthy behaviours.

Studies have demonstrated that viewing pictures of a romantic partner reduced experimental pain due to the activation of the neural reward systems in the brain. A number of studies across the globe have all concluded that acts of kindness and altruism towards others reduced chronic pain

---

[8] Social Relationships and Mortality Risk: A Meta-analytic Review - Julianne Holt-Lunstad, Timothy B. Smith, J. Bradley Layton - Social Relationships and Mortality Risk: A Meta-analytic Review Published: July 27, 2010
https://doi.org/10.1371/journal.pmed.1000316

and in one case the pain relief induced by doing things for others was over twice as affective as medicinal pain relief.

We are physically, emotionally and psychologically designed to work more efficiently when we are connected to others.

Physical connection:

The proven links between human connection and improved wellbeing extend to physical contact also. Tactile stimulation can trigger the body to release oxytocin, the 'love' hormone. It also lowers cortisol levels, reducing anxiety and stress. This doesn't only apply to romantic skin to skin contact or touch from a partner. Any touch can have huge health benefits and has been shown to alleviate depression, improve immune function, reduce pain, enhance attentiveness, decrease blood pressure and calm the heart rate. It speeds recovery times from illness and surgery, aids digestion and boosts survival rates of patients with complex diseases. When aggressive teenagers are given massages, anxiety and aggression decrease. Alzheimer's patients do better with regular nurturing touch therapies such as massage. It seems that much can be credited to a type of nerve fibre on the skin called the CT afferent nerve fibre, which is sensitive to gentle stroking. These touch-sensitive nerve fibres known as C tactile fibres, convey a pleasant sensation when activated, which is conducted to the brain's limbic system (via signals from sensory neutrons) to the central nervous system. Astonishingly, these fibres are optimally stimulated when you stroke the skin at 3–5 cms per second. This tends to be the rate at which parents stroke their children, quite automatically.

This touch, which is designed to be comforting and nurturing, is completely instinctive in parents. There is an emotional quality to that type of touch. Stimulation of CT nerve fibres lowers the heart rate, increases oxytocin and increases the amount of natural T-cells (which help the body fight viruses and other pathogens) in the body. Researchers have measured immune function in healthy adults who were massaged for 45 minutes[9]. The massaged group had substantially more white blood cells including the natural killer T-cells and fewer types of inflammatory cytokines associated with autoimmune diseases than their 'unmassaged' counterparts. Even days after the massaging had finished, the benefit continued.

All of these things associated with increased wellbeing are influenced by human connection and human touch. It is no surprise that psychologists are warning of the future impact of lockdown and social distancing measures being implemented to manage the COVID19 pandemic. Community and touch is essential to good holistic health.

Self-care and self-love:

In the western world, we focus very much on teaching our toddlers practical self-care skills such as toileting, how to clean their teeth, dress themselves and so on. These are, of course, important skills which enable development of

---

[9] A Preliminary Study of the Effects of Repeated Massage on Hypothalamic–Pituitary–Adrenal and Immune Function in Healthy Individuals: A Study of Mechanisms of Action and Dosage - Mark H. Rapaport, MD, Pamela Schettler, PhD and Catherine Bresee, MS2
https://www.ncbi.nlm.nih.gov/pmc/articles/PMC3419840/

independent living and a sense of self accomplishment and self-worth. Equally important, however, are the psychological skills needed for effective self-care in our adult lives. These skills, especially skills relating to positive psychological self-care, depend upon healthy attachment to our caregivers and reinforcement of self-confidence and self-esteem as we grow. Very often disrupted attachments in our childhood or life experiences that damage our self-esteem or self-confidence result in us being unable to meet our own needs and to become focused on prioritising the needs of others. We may never have been taught how to properly make assessments about what is good for us or indeed how to assess or to take risks in a safe way. As we reinforce feelings of low self-worth over time, we are likely to attract others into our lives who will take advantage of our unhealthy behaviour and low self-esteem. This kind of treatment by others together with our own conduct towards ourselves reinforces our lack of self-worth even more and so the problem worsens. It is fairly easy to notice the signs of not taking care of ourselves physically but it's much more difficult to recognise that we are not practicing good emotional or psychological self-care. Very few of us are taught how to offer ourselves praise when things go well or to feel positively about prioritising our own needs over the needs of others. It is even more difficult to recognise when we have stopped respecting or loving ourselves, which can often be seen through the way that we behave towards others or in the way that we allow ourselves to be treated. It becomes habitual and, therefore, much more difficult to notice because it is our 'norm'.

    Emotional self-care and self-love are psychologically complex subjects. The reasons for failing to look after ourselves are unique to each person and are widely varied. In order to be able to consistently practice better self-care in all areas, it is helpful to identify the reasons that apply to you, possibly with the help of a psychologist or other trained professional. Whatever the level of self-awareness it is important for each of us to recognise the positives in ourselves and to feel proud of who we are.

There may be many things causing us to believe that we don't deserve better. Whether we believe it or not, one way to change the downwards spiral of negative beliefs is to start behaving in a different way. This changes the direction of the spiral upwards into a more positive sphere, which in turn helps us to behave even more positively and so the cycle continues. Taking a short amount of time each day, if possible, or each week to do something that you enjoy should kick-start positive change. Be fiercely protective of that 'me' time and do not say yes to anything that will cause you to lose it! Even five minutes can make a huge difference if set aside daily.

Regular physical exercise and mediation / yoga practice have been shown to improve our feelings of positivity and self-worth, too. Identifying something that we like about ourselves and focusing on that whilst we are brushing our teeth each morning and night is another option. By choosing a positive activity to engage in whilst we do something that we are already in the habit of doing every day helps to maintain consistency and regularity (habit stacking). It doesn't have to be a big change, just a small one that can be sustained for two weeks to habit form, at which point commitment will be fortified and a second change can be stacked on top.

Part of building our self-esteem is centred in having faith in ourselves to make the right choice and then having the confidence and authority to implement those decisions. In our very busy modern lives, it is essential to recognise that we can do anything with time and dedication but we cannot do everything all at once. Part of looking after our physical and mental health, therefore, becomes about choosing what we allow into our lives and how we expend our time and energy. The importance of saying 'no' and meaning it, creating and holding our own boundaries, is essential to developing self-esteem. We have to start treating ourselves with the respect that we would wish to receive from others. Some support may be required in identifying the right direction for change but usually these signposts come from a 'gut feeling' about what is right for us. Indicators may be centred in a deep feeling of discomfort or unhappiness in continuing with certain behaviour or experiences that are unhealthy or which just no longer fit.

In Western societies we have become so disconnected from our 'gut feelings that we have lost faith in our ability to make intuitive decisions. Our societal obsession with 'evidence-based' decision making has caused us to outsource our decision making to others who we perceive to 'know better' than we do. We may have become disconnected from our ability to make intuitive decisions but the power to reconnect remains available to us. The gut will never make a bad or unsafe decision. It is not clouded by conditioning or ego as the brain is! It never over-thinks or over-complicates anything. In a process of developing self-trust and self-belief, listening out for that voice of intuition is a great start. Somatic healing work or yoga are two simple ways to really grapple with the body-mind disconnect and start living as one again.

Reconnecting with our authenticity, building self-confidence and having trust and belief in who we each individually are is one of the most valuable self-care processes available. We must trust that we are capable of making change, of knowing what feels right and have courage in ourselves to make those changes and sustain them in the face of any objections from others. It can be done but it takes decisiveness and determination, trust and belief, all of which we all already have within us.

Self-care and self-love is not selfish. Placing ourselves at the forefront is sometimes necessary. By ignoring our own needs, we tell ourselves such a lot about how much value we place on ourselves and the kind of treatment that we expect and allow from others. If we cannot love ourselves, how do we expect to love anyone else or be loved in a respectful way? A journey into wellbeing, all starts with self-love.

As Audre Lorde so eloquently said,

"Caring for myself is not self-indulgence, its self-preservation"

Unconscious Absorption:

Our minds work on two levels at all times: the conscious and the subconscious. The conscious mind controls the things that we do that we are aware of. Reading this page and understanding it are conscious acts, for example. However, the subconscious mind is always hard at work making sense of the words you absorb and comparing it to what we already believe that we know about the world, mostly informed by our previous life experiences. Our subconscious mind begins absorbing information from the moment that we are born. We have no prior knowledge base when we are an infant and simply tuck away everything that we experience as being valid and true. This is the belief system that we hold in our subconscious hard drive and is the framework upon which the rest of our life is lived, unless it is reprogrammed. For example, if you were made to feel that you were ugly when you were little, that becomes your programming. We will continue to believe this and should we be approached romantically by someone who is attractive in later life, we may perceive this to be a cruel trick or joke. We, therefore, sabotage what could be a positive relationship or experience based upon our subconscious belief that we are not attractive enough.

"As you sow in your subconscious mind, so shall you reap in your body and environment." – Joseph Murphy

Unfortunately, because the subconscious mind operates below the level of consciousness, it takes awareness, positive effort and persistence to re-programme. The good news is that it absolutely can be done through repetitive positive reinforcement over time in a variety of ways, including:

1. Changing our environment

The subconscious mind absorbs information constantly without us ever being aware of it, until something triggers a reaction. If our daily environment is full of negativity and strife, our mind will absorb this and use it to reinforce negative beliefs about ourselves. To change our mind set to a more positive one, we should strictly limit the negativity we expose ourselves to. This requires constant awareness and commitment to remove ourselves from a negative environment. This becomes easier to do as we practice positive reinforcement.

"Whatever we plant in our subconscious mind and nourish with repetition and emotion will one day become a reality" – Earl Nightingale

2. Affirmations and visualisation

Repeated positive affirmations practiced regularly each day out loud if possible are absorbed forcefully by the subconscious mind and over time, our thinking about ourselves begins to align with those affirmations. Visualisation has the same effect. The more vivid the visualisation is, the more persuasive it becomes to the subconscious mind. When visualising what we want from life, we should make the scene as real as possible. Notice tiny details, how does the scene smell and feel? Both affirmations and visualisation are most effective if we are in a relaxed state, perhaps during a period of mindfulness or after meditation or when just waking from sleep. Morning affirmations also have the benefit of setting the tone for the day, making it more likely that we will be mindful and aware of maintaining a positive environment around us and helping us to avoid negative thoughts. Creating a positive mindset actually changes the chemical and hormonal composition of the body. The impact is profound!

3. Neuro Linguistic Programming

NLP can be used for personal development, phobias and anxiety. NLP uses perceptual, behavioural and communication techniques to make it easier for people to change their thoughts and actions. NLP relies on language processing and so is performed when in a conscious state but with the objective of changing the subconscious mind.

4. Hypnosis

During hypnosis, the hypnotist gradually moves the mind into a more relaxed and receptive state and then delivers positive and empowering messages to the subconscious mind to achieve the desired objective. Self-hypnosis can also be undertaken by using pre-recorded messages. Anxiety about hypnosis can be overcome by simply recording our own voice, reciting positive affirmations to be played as we go to sleep or whilst we are in a relaxed state.

Love and kindness:

Part of reprogramming our mind set is learning to believe that we deserve love and kindness in all things, both consciously and subconsciously, to create a genuinely held belief that we are deserving of the best of everything. This involves treating ourselves with love and kindness in everything that we do, in everything that we think and in every decision that we make. We can create this environment for ourselves by behaving this way towards others, too. By living in a way that is driven by love and positivity, we create that environment for ourselves and develop that mind-set as a habit. It becomes our version of normal. We learn to expect nothing less from others than that which we are giving to ourselves. We improve our future by improving our present. It is a simple proposition but it works and is so simple to begin. As we already know, giving to and helping others gives us a physical feel-good factor which is physically as well as psychologically real. This behaviour is even more impactive when directed inwards, towards the self.

Connection to all things:

The principles of quantum physics and quantum mechanics teach that everything in the universe is connected in some way to everything else. It is not necessary to be physically touching something to be deeply connected to it. Everything on earth and in space is made of matter which is vibrating at different frequencies. Things which vibrate at similar frequencies are attracted or drawn to one another. As humans, our vibrational level varies depending upon our mood and presentation. In accepting this connection to all things, we become more grounded and rooted in our lives and feel more secure in our place in the world. A sense of connection also motivates the mind to take care of others and of our natural world and also to perceive our environment as a friendly rather than a hostile place. This creates a positive emotional and psychological environment in which to progress towards a better sense of balance and in which to achieve healthy and meaningful personal growth.

Taking care of the heart:

Whilst Western cultures perceive the brain to be the driving force of the body, in fact, there is emerging evidence which suggests that the heart has a crucial role to play outside of beating blood and oxygen around our circulatory system. This has been an accepted principle of Eastern culture and medicine for thousands of years. Those traditions credit the heart with holding instinctive knowledge about what our ancestors have experienced and the best path in life for us to take. The heart is thought to be deeply connected to our life force. The 'life force' or soul that makes us unique and which is believed in many culture to arrive in our body at birth and leave it at the time of our death is known as 'Chi' or 'Qi' in China, 'Mana' in Polynesia and 'Prana' in India. In the West, Dr Wilhelm Reich discovered the same energy and called it Orgone energy. It is known as Bio-Plasmic Energy by Russian researchers. The understanding that our bodies are filled with life force energy that is directly connected to the quality of our health has been part of the wisdom of these cultures for thousands of years and has resulted in the development of many different forms of alternative therapies such as acupuncture and reflexology, Yoga, Tai Chi – these are all subtle energetic practices as well as physical practices. In separating the heart's role in western medicine, its importance is often overlooked and the messages that it tries to tell us through our intuition or 'the little voice in our head' or 'gut feelings' are often ignored.

In his book *The Heart's Code*, Paul Pearsall PhD[10] offers 'Essential health warnings' to maintain a healthy heart balance. He describes how modern living has elevated the brain to the 'decision maker' rather than 'going with our gut' or 'following our intuition'. He notes that the brain is tied to our ego and so constantly pushes us to do more, to have more, to be dissatisfied with what we already have and to be in competition with others. He notes that this way of living leaves us disconnected and isolated and incapable of achieving our potential as a result. He urges us to consider new ways of understanding our own responsibilities, limitations and emotional impacts on others. He encourages us to change this distorted way of living by trying to tune in once again to the messages that our heart provides about how to live well and in line with our intended purpose. He offers the following suggestions to achieve this objective, which is also excellent advice for anyone intending to reduce their anxiety levels, blood pressure and other physical stressors or to improve the quality of their connections with others:

1. Don't abuse your heart by allowing your brain to physically harm it by exposing it to constant stress and straining towards self-fulfilment.
2. Don't exploit your heart by allowing your brain to misappropriate its miraculous energy for selfish purposes.

---

[10] The Heart's Code: Tapping the Power and Wisdom of our Heart Energy, Dr Paul Pearsall, April 1999

3. Don't deprive your heart by allowing our brain's innate selfishness to distance you from the hearts of others.
4. Don't neglect your heart by allowing your brain to be so busily and reactively consumed with trying to stay alive that it forgets to allow time for your heart to proactively reflect on what purposes you chose for living.

Loving what we have:

We cannot change the behaviour of others, only our own conduct. We cannot always change what happens to us but we are fully in control of our response to it. We can choose whether to live in a negative and automated environment or in a positive and conscious one. We can choose where to set our own limits and expectations. We can choose whether to continue to strive for more or to enjoy what we have. We can choose whether to love ourselves or to treat ourselves cruelly. We can choose whether to see the world as a hostile and aggressive place, full of danger and risk or a loving place full of opportunity and positivity. If we choose to try and see the world through loving and compassionate eyes, we are much more likely to see and enjoy the positive experiences that life has to offer and to be better placed to manage the trials and challenges of life in a healthy and balanced way.

MANTRA for self-love: I love and I am loved

Reflection:

Think of a negative experience that you have recently caused by someone else. What happened? How did you respond? What consequences flowed from your response? Who is to blame for the consequences that finally flowed? Is it the person who caused the negativity towards you or were you responsible for reacting in the way that you did? Are you able to accept your part in what happened?

If you cannot accept any responsibility, it may be helpful to know that this kind of reaction is often displayed by someone who feels disempowered that they have no control over their own life.

How much control do you believe you have over your own life? Are there things that you want to be able to control but cannot? What are they? How could you take control over those things? What options do you have? In a perfect world, how would you want to manage this situation? What is stopping you from doing so? What fear do you have about taking those steps?

Think about the negative situation identified at the outset of this reflection. How could you have responded differently? How might that have changed the final outcome? Would it have left your feeling more or less empowered?

Finally, think about how much time you spend being kind to yourself during the course of a typical day. Note down anything that you do today which is positive for you (not for others) and how much time that takes up. Write it here:

There are 1,440 minutes in a day. Do you think that you have spent enough of those being kind to yourself? How can you increase that number tomorrow?

Chapter 7
Mindfulness

Rushing around and trying to fit too much into an already busy day is a regrettable feature of modern living. It can be exhausting. Our lives are overflowing with responsibility and accountability and our heads are constantly thinking about the next task on the never ending list of things we have to do. In the rush to accomplish so much during each day, many of us worry about the quality of our output, whether it be in relationships, our professional lives or in our role as a parent. Living in this way can be damaging to our health, undermining of our self-esteem and contrary to any regime of self-care. When we live in this pattern, we cannot possibly offer our best output in anything or feel good about what we achieve.

The old adage of multi-tasking is a myth. Our brain does not function with a dual core processor. It has one processor – your mind. In order to try to manage multiple tasks at any given time, the brain has to rapidly switch between them. This is tiring for the brain as it requires greater energy and concentration per minute than when focusing on one task. 'Switching' is also unlikely to derive the same levels of output that we could achieve if we focussed on just one thing. At the same time as asking our brains to switch, the stressful modern life brings the need to manage a deluge of information – emails, telephone calls, texts, social media messages and distractions. Home life brings with it the demands of others in our household as well as our own expectations and commitments. Thinking about what we have and have not done and what still needs to be done and constant fretting about the quality of our performance leads to frustration and anxiety. The result is a life which, for the most part, is spent in one place doing one thing whilst thinking about something completely different. We are rarely emmersed in the present moment completely.

When we live our lives in this fog of distraction, thinking either about what we have already done or what we have yet to do, we miss the detail of the reality around us. Imagine living life in a slightly frosted glass box: we experience what we are doing without any of the 'feels', we miss the smells and sounds, we miss the beauty and the joy. We miss the glorious detail and the lessons that the experience would ordinarily bring. This is stifling to self-development and awareness and can be very isolating. The life we live becomes one that takes place in our heads as we limit the true and meaningful interactions with those around us. As we become increasingly caught up in our own thoughts, we lose our ability to identify and manage how that thinking influences what we feel and how we behave. We lose our awareness and in doing so, we gradually lose control over our self-development and internal experience.

The bad news is that it is very easy to fall into this trap of mindless living, missing the only moment that ever truly exists in reality, which is the present moment or the 'now'.

The good news is that it is relatively easy to start to shift our thinking back to consciousness, through the practice of mindfulness. Mindfulness requires some simple changes to the way that we choose to live. A regular mindfulness practice promotes awareness of every element of our lives as it happens and so increases our enjoyment and appreciation of the present moment.

In order for the mind to rest from its distractions of the past and future, it must learn to reconnect with the body and refocus on the self. Disconnecting from the fast-paced life we lead and reconnecting with self is not easy to start with. As with any new skill it takes practice to become a habit but it can be done! As we start to learn anything, the brain builds new neurological pathways to enable that new activity to become easier over time. The more we use those pathways, the more established they become, a little bit like walking through deep snow or a field of crops. The first time we create the new pathway, the second time we follow it slowly and re-establish its course, the third time the path is a little easier to see and follow and so on until eventually, we can skip down the track without having to think about it at all.

Mindfulness is developed in the pre-frontal cortex. This is the 'newer,' evolutionary part of our brains that helps us to resist temptation, maintain focus and strategically plan. Just as with any other part of our body, it is possible to train this area to become stronger and more dominant. Strengthening the pre-frontal cortex will enable it to overcome the draw of the more primitive parts of the brain. These older and more primitive parts, such as the basal ganglia, condition us in old habits and behaviours and tempt us into ideas of familiarity (which as humans we usually find comforting, even if they are not healthy or good for us!) Every time we engage in new behaviour, we build and strengthen the relevant neuro pathways and so we make the new pattern more robust and established, therefore, make it an easier and more naturally attractive path.

Regularly making conscious decisions to redirect the brain and thought patterns also trains us to understand that we are in control over all that we think and do and gives us the skills and confidence to develop healthier thinking patterns. For example, if we constantly think about something that makes us angry, the brain fortifies the pathways for angry thinking patterns. This makes the brain adept at thinking in an angry way and we become drawn into that thinking pattern more frequently. Often we think that the only way to stop feeling angry is to resolve the issue that prompted that feeling. In fact, that is not correct. If we decide that we will no longer feel angry about it anymore and consciously switch our thinking pattern to something more positive, we can also stop ourselves from feeling angry, even if the original event is still happening. The ability to re-frame our thinking is the ultimate product of mindfulness.

How to start living more mindfully:

Start small for best results. When you leave the house or when you leave work, take a few minutes to notice how you feel. Perhaps the car journey that you usually spend worrying about the day ahead could be used to think about how you feel or what is around you or who the people are that pass you on the street or on the tube. How does your coffee smell? Are you warm? Cold? Tired? Hungry? Try to set a time each day within your usual routine when you will stop, reconnect with self and focus on how you feel. After a few days, this will become much easier and you are likely to start noticing these things about yourself at other times, too, without any effort.

Once you have introduced yourself to the concept of mindfulness, try adding a little more into your daily routine at different times of the day. This will train your brain to be more aware and so more mindful in a more natural and constant way rather than having to plan for it. A good method is to choose an activity that you regularly engage in through the day. Perhaps you might choose taking a drink or a frequently used example in mindfulness training, opening a door. In the former example, each time you take a drink of something, be aware of it. Thankfully, actually doing this is not as odd as it might sound! Notice what you are drinking? Why are you drinking it? Are you thirsty or is it a social reason? Is it a habit that you have unknowingly created over the years, maybe for caffeine or alcohol? What is the temperature of your drink? How does the cup feel in your hand? How does it taste? Do you like it? How does it feel in your mouth and how does it make your body feel when you swallow it? The answers to these questions are available each time we take a drink but we never notice them because we don't stop to do so. We don't fully immerse ourselves in these routine experiences. A simple act of making time to notice the first sip of each drink we take through the day or any other task will begin to create new habits within our brains and get our new neuro pathways, firing up and building strength. As we develop the habit of greater awareness, other things will begin to be enjoyed in different and more meaningful ways too.

It is useful to practice disconnecting from the everyday stresses and refocusing on self. Guided meditations are an excellent way to notice when attention is being diverted and a great way to start a habit of disconnection from the distraction of external factors. The guidance in meditation helps us to notice when our minds have wandered and prompt us to bring attention back to what we are doing. New practitioners cannot fail to be astonished by how quickly the mind wanders back to what you have to do before bedtime or what is for dinner! The mind-set that a mindfulness practice creates is one where we start to accept that everything passes and nothing is forever. Just as the trees let go of their leaves in Autumn, so our thoughts and experiences will also pass. The same is true of relationships, jobs, heartbreak and joy. All of this passes and is momentary and that is to be expected. Understanding and accepting this concept helps us to detach and not to cling on to things which are no longer of benefit. Regular mindfulness practice increases the ability to let go and allow things to pass through. It increases the ability to focus as new neuro pathways become established and our awareness and ability to master this new skill continues to grow.

The breath is a powerful tool in the quest to rebalance and refocus if we know how to use it. Breathing is the cornerstone of mindfulness and many other self-care practices for very good reason and it can be used to quickly regain composure, reset our biochemical balance and centre our thoughts. Do you remember you parent or teacher telling you to 'take a deep breath' if you were very upset, had hurt yourself or were panicking? When we make any change to our ordinary subconscious pattern of breathing, we are forced to be mindful of it. Our focus immediately shifts inward and we become distracted from what is happening around us, concentrating on the breath. Our single core processor of a brain is focussed only on the breath and so we feel much more in control almost immediately. Breathing exercises are an extremely useful tool in stress management. Another example of this inward shift is when we were told as children to count to ten if we were feeling angry to prevent emotional retaliation. Again, our focus shifts inward and distracts us from what is making us angry and enabling us to be conscious and in control of our emotional response rather than reacting with our limbic, stressed and ego-driven subconscious brain.

Using the breath to maintain concentration on ourselves and so become more mindful is easy because the breath is always in the present. It cannot be the last breath you took because that has passed. It cannot be the breath that is coming next because that is and will always be in the future. The only breath that matters is the one we are taking now. It is a very potent symbol of being present and focussing upon it will help you to take back control of those racing thoughts. Breathing exercises are an amazing way to take the sting out of stress in seconds.

As previously mentioned, mindfulness is hinged in the concept that everything is transient. Nothing stays forever. Just as our breath comes and goes to be replaced with the new, so our relationships come and go, our present life will one day pass too. Mindfulness teaches us to accept that we cannot hold onto things forever but that this is OK and we could manage without anything that is currently in our lives if we have to. It builds resilience and reduces reliance upon external factors. One day, whatever we are holding onto will pass and make space for new things to experience and enjoy. Mindfulness encourages us to have confidence in ourselves and to acknowledge that we are resourceful and capable and in fact, we already have all that we need to live well. Once we are accepting of the principles that (a) We cannot control everything that surrounds us and that (b) We can confidently let the things that surround us go and that we will still be OK, it becomes so much easier to let worries dissolve. When we find ourselves being distracted by worries or outside thought whilst practicing mindfulness or other self-care practices such as yoga or meditation, it becomes second nature to let it pass through our conscious thinking. All mindfulness practitioners will become distracted from time to time and that is OK and is to be expected. Noticing when you have become distracted during a mindfulness practice and letting it floating away is a useful practice in everyday life too, especially in managing stress. The greatest advantage is that this can be done anywhere that we become distracted or begin to worry whether it be on the train, at work or in the queue at the checkout.

Part of the stress in modern life is self-made. We apply so much pressure to ourselves in setting expectations unrealistically high, whether that be in terms of performance, ability or how much we can cram into one finite day. We are so impatient with ourselves and rarely recognise our achievements. We expect everything to be done immediately. We want to see tangible, meaningful change straight away. These unhelpful habits have accumulated over many years. It will take time and patience to undo and unpick them. Some changes will be felt immediately but the practice of unconscious mindfulness takes time to unfold. Persistence and commitment to self-improvement and better wellbeing is key.

In any journey towards better wellbeing, it is important that we brace ourselves for change. It is the experience of almost everyone who practises mindfulness that change for the better does come. Living in a more mindful way cannot help but bring enjoyment in new things and also makes us aware of practices and habits that we have developed which no longer bring any happiness. As we transition, we must have courage and faith in ourselves to persevere. The goal is to get rid of the things that no longer bring joy or benefit to make space for those which will.

If you are reading this book then you deserve the utmost respect for the changes that you are contemplating to better your life. Respect the decision that you are making for self-improvement. Give the process the time that it deserves. Make it a priority and persevere, just as you would if you were trying to lose weight or study for a new qualification. Self-empowerment and self-care is a lifestyle. It's not a switch that can be flicked on and off. It takes time to develop the practice of mindfulness but once it is established and the impact of greater awareness starts to be felt, you will never want to switch it off again.

MANTRA for mindful living: I am present in every moment of life.

Mindfulness Exercise:

Start by finding a quiet or comfortable place to sit or lie down. Try to find a place which is as quiet as possible. When you are ready, either close your eyes or soften your gaze, trying not to let the eyes wander. Imagine yourself lying in a beautiful summer field of flowers and soft grass. Try to feel the sun shining and warming your face and body. Imagine looking skyward and seeing birds and white clouds passing through the blue sky above. Relax. Notice how you feel in your mind but also check in with different parties of your body, starting with each feature of the face and working down to the toes. Aim to remain here for at least five minutes. During this time, notice as thoughts wander into your mind. They will come and that's OK. Without any frustration or judgment, encourage those thoughts to float away and return your concentration to the blue sky and sunshine above. As you practice this task more frequently, you will find that your thoughts wander less, it becomes easier to get rid of any that do appear and you can remain in this relaxed state for longer and longer. So many helpful guided meditations are available online or in group classes.

Breathing Exercises:

The easiest exercise to access is the counting of breath and particularly square breathing. Inhale deeply and slowly to the count of four, hold for four, exhale for four and hold for four before repeating. As you feel your body and mind calm, slow the counting and take longer, deeper breaths. This is an exercise that can be done anywhere, eyes open or closed. If you keep your eyes open, try to soften your gaze and not let the eyes wander.

To instantly promote calm, inhale through the nose for a count of four and exhale through the mouth for seven. As you repeat, slow the breath and relax the body.

For an instant energy boost, take a deep inhalation through the nose and rapidly force the breath out of the nostrils once per second for up to a minute. Finish with a deep inhalation and relax.

Chapter 8
Breathing for Beginners

If there is one essential part of life that we almost all take for granted, it is our breath? We rarely give it a second thought and yet life itself always starts and ends with the breath.

Breathing is a primary function of the 'reptilian' brain (the brain stem and cerebellum), which is the area of the brain in charge of essential functions that we don't need to think about. As well as breathing, these primary functions include our heart rate, temperature and balance. It is these functions of the reptilian brain which ensure our survival as individuals and also as a species. Our life is considered in law to begin when we take our first breath. That first intake of oxygen under our own instruction signals the beginning of the existence of us as a new individual, capable of surviving independently, outside of the comfort and safety of the womb. At the moment of birth, the entire cast of the delivery suite is focussed on that first breath. Once it has been gasped and is regulated, the focus shifts to other things. The automatic function of the breath has been kick started and we assume that it will continue in its reliable pattern.

We rarely give it a second thought.

We recognise that there are variations in our breathing patterns from time to time. For example, we probably notice that our breathing becomes quicker when we are excited, stressed or under pressure. Conversely, the breath is slower and tends to be deeper when we are sleeping or relaxed or when we are very focussed. We understand that the body forces us to yawn, to take in more oxygen, when we are tired and our breathing may have become shallow and lethargic through habit. The pattern of our breath is often dictated by our mood or our physical state. What so many of us fail to appreciate is that we can use this strong connection and interplay between our psychological state, physical state and the breath to change our mood and mind-set as well as to make changes to the physical body and regulate the autonomic nervous system.

Through the breath, we inhale the oxygen that our bodies need to function. We breath in about 17,000 times per day. The vital organs including the gut, brain, bones, blood and heart work hard together to deliver oxygen to tissue around the body. Our brain stem initiates breathing through messages through our nervous system to the diaphragm and ribs, telling these areas to contract. As they do so, the lungs expand. This expansion reduces internal pressure in the lung cavities and allows air to rush in. As we inhale, the oxygen molecules contained within the air are absorbed through the walls of the lungs and then transported around the body to where oxygen is required, carried by our red blood cells which are made by the food we eat.

Chemical and mechanical digestion breaks down our food into the different vitamins and minerals that the body requires. In the making of red blood cells, iron is king. Our kidneys regulate the release of these newly made red blood cells into the bloodstream at an astonishing rate of around 2.5 million cells per second. The red blood cells carry the oxygen through the cardio vascular network to every cell in body. Our highly complex system of blood vessels if measured end to end would wrap around earth several times. The responsibility of pushing the blood cells and oxygen around this vast network belongs falls the heart, which pumps an average of 100,000 times per day to get the oxygen to where it needs to go.

In controlling our breath, we are, therefore, controlling the amount of oxygen in our bodies, our heart rate and the speed at which our other vital organs function.

The physical impact of controlling the breath is quite remarkable. When we slow the breath, we also reduce our heart rate, switch on our parasympathetic nervous system and boost our immune system. This results in some unexpected benefits such as:

Dulling pain:

Breathing deeply causes the body to releases endorphins, which are the feel good hormones and a natural pain killer created by the body itself.

Improved blood flow:

The deeper the breath, the greater the movement of the diaphragm upwards and downwards. This helps remove toxins from the body and promotes better blood flow.

Increasing energy levels:

As the blood flow increases with deeper breath, we take more oxygen into our blood, resulting in increased energy levels.

Detoxification:

Shallow breathing makes it more difficult for the body to expel toxic carbon dioxide effectively. As a result, our 'back-up' detoxification system starts working harder to expel it. Over time, this brings stress to the body that is not designed to be sustained over time.

Improving posture:

Believe it or not, bad posture is related to incorrect breathing. Try breathing deeply and notice how your body starts to straighten up during the process. When you fill your lungs with air, this automatically encourages the spine to straighten to its proper alignment.

Stimulating lymphatic system:

The lymphatic drainage system is a network of tissues and organs that help rid the body of toxins, waste and other unwanted materials. The main role of the lymphatic system is to transport lymph, a fluid containing the powerful, infection-fighting white blood cells throughout the body. Shallow breathing can lead to a sluggish lymphatic system which will not detoxify properly. Deep breathing will help get the lymph flowing properly so that the body can work more efficiently and keep inflammation down.

Improving digestion:

Breathing deeply supplies more oxygen to all of our body parts including our digestive system. A greater flow of oxygen helps it to work more efficiently and improve overall digestion. In addition, deep breathing promotes a calm and better regulated nervous system, so also promoting optimal digestion.

Activation of the parasympathetic nervous system:

The sympathetic nervous system (sometimes known as the fight or flight response) was intended as a survival mechanism to allow us to react quickly to a situation that was life-threatening. Unfortunately, today the human body has the same response to non-life-threatening stressors that cause high levels of anxiety, releasing corticotrophic and adrenocorticotropic hormones including cortisol that keep the body on high alert and ready for intense physical activity.

We know from a vast amount of research that the long-term effects of chronic stress affect a person's psychological and physical health. According to an article in Harvard Health Publishing entitled *Understanding the Stress Response*,[11]

"The repeated activation of the stress response takes a toll on the body. Research suggests that chronic stress contributes to high blood pressure, promotes the formation of artery-clogging deposits and causes brain changes that may

---

[11] https://www.health.harvard.edu/staying.healthy/understanding-the-stress-response

contribute to anxiety, depression and addiction. More preliminary research suggests that chronic stress may also contribute to obesity, both through direct mechanisms (causing people to eat more) or indirectly (decreasing sleep and exercise)."

To switch off the sympathetic nervous system (the stress response), we must activate the parasympathetic nervous system. This works to relax and slow down the body's responses. Once a perceived threat has passed, the body's cortisol levels reduce. The parasympathetic nervous system slows the stress response by releasing hormones that relax the mind and body and slow down the high energy functions. Switching on the parasympathetic nervous system immediately reduces anxiety and stress. Conscious breathing, more slowly and deeply, quickly achieves a sense of relaxation, lifts the mood, strengthens the immune system and reduces blood pressure.

Consciously using the breath to change these physical and psychological patterns in the body is extremely powerful. Breathing practices can very quickly help us to regain a sense of self control and empowerment. It is an extremely effective tool for anyone trying to change unhelpful patterns of behaviour such as addiction, anger management or self-sabotage. Breathing is the best and quickest way to bring the stress response down. Taking fewer breaths, moving as slowly as possible from one breath to next brings almost instant calm to body and mind and an inwards shift in focus. By prolonging every breath and inhaling more deeply and exhaling fully, it is possible to balance carbon-dioxide and oxygen levels and quickly reduce blood pressure.

Conscious breath can also benefit the body when stretching. In any stretch or yoga position, bringing conscious deep breathing to the party will enhance the stretch without placing the body under any additional physical stress. This helps to create space in the body by releasing muscular tension and constriction without strain or risk of tissue or ligament damage.

Breathing practices may help to enhance the effectiveness of your breathing. For some people with conditions that affect their lung function, bringing this awareness to daily routines may help improve the sensation of breathing and as a result, their daily activities.

The focus that conscious breathing brings enables us to quiet the mind and focus on what is internal rather than the external noise that we constantly live with in modern times. The ability to screen out the noise is essential to finding peace and balance in a busy, stressful world.

MANTRA for breathwork: Breathe in positivity, breathe out negativity

Exercise:

Some easy breathing practices to improve a greater sense of health and wellbeing in everyone are:

- **Slow breath:** Slow the breath to the 'optimal' level by inhaling for a count of five seconds and exhaling for five seconds. Repeat for at least one minute, increasing the time each day.

- **Deep diaphragmatic breathing:** Breathe in slowly and deeply through the nose, concentrating awareness on the breath entering the body. Notice as it travels through the nose into the throat and down towards the belly. Breathe right into the belly filling it completely. Exhale through the mouth using the same process, being mindful of the breath leaving the body and tracking its path. It is helpful to do this exercise whilst sitting straight and upright or lying flat, either way keep the spine straight and aligned. It may also help to place one hand on the chest and the other on the belly to more easily track the path of the breath, attune mind and body and maintain focus on the exercise.

Reflection:

Next time you are in a heightened state of emotion, turn your attention to your breath. Try to notice how you are breathing; shallow or deeply, fast or slow. Is there tightness anywhere in your chest, back, shoulders? Do you notice anything elsewhere in the body? How does your head feel? What is your temperature? Notice how you feel physically and emotionally. Then shift the focus to one of the breathing exercises above. How does that change the things that you had noticed before? How quickly do these changes take effect? How much more in control do you feel?

Chapter 9
Sleep Stories

It is only in the last decade or two that scientists have become more aware of the importance of sleep and the impact upon our general health and wellbeing of not having enough of it. We now know that sleep is a fundamental part of maintaining optimal mind-body function and that sleep deprivation has a significant impact upon us, far wider and more deeply than we have ever appreciated before. A lack of sleep can be caused by internal factors such as stress or other physical condition like pain or sleep apnea or by external factors such as our daytime activities or our sleeping environment. Not all of these factors are within our control but whatever the cause, there is always positive action that can be taken to improve our sleep hygiene and so positively impact our health.

During sleep, the brain moves through five different stages. One of these stages is rapid eye movement (REM) sleep. During this phase, the eyes move rapidly in various directions. The other four phases are referred to as non-REM (NREM) sleep. REM sleep occurs several times nightly. It accounts for approximately 20–25% of an adult's sleep cycle and over 50% of an infant's. Most dreams occur during REM sleep and it is thought to play a role in learning, memory and mood. Before entering the REM sleep phase, the body goes through each of the stages of NREM sleep. In Stage 1 NREM sleep, we are in a state of very light sleep. Stage 2 NREM sleep is a slightly deeper sleep. Body temperature drops and heart rate slows down. Stages 3 and 4 NREM sleep are a state of deep and restorative sleep known as slow wave sleep or delta sleep. The muscles relax, the supply of blood to the muscles increases and the body repairs and grows tissue. Hormones are released and energy stores are replenished. The brain shuts off from outside stimulus, promoting complete rest. We need both NREM and REM sleep to remain healthy. During NREM sleep, the brain clears out and rebuilds neuro pathways and in REM phase sleep, they are consolidated and strengthened.

Recent studies have shown that chronic or long term sleep restriction, however minor, can be just as impactive on our cognitive performance as shorter term or one-off periods of total sleep deprivation[12]. Whereas total sleep deprivation affects long-term memory and decision making, working memory and attention (especially vigilance) is affected just as much by long term sleep restriction. This makes driving or operating heavy machinery especially dangerous after a long

---

[12] Sleep deprivation: Impact on cognitive performance - Paula Alhola and Päivi Polo-Kantola 2007
https://www.ncbi.nlm.nih.gov/pmc/articles/PMC2656292/
Short- and long-term health consequences of sleep disruption - Goran Medic, Micheline Wille and Michiel EH Hemels 2017
https://www.ncbi.nlm.nih.gov/pmc/articles/PMC5449130/
Sleep duration and cognition: is there an ideal amount? - Janna Mantua, Guido Simonelli 2019
https://academic.oup.com/sleep/article/42/3/zsz010/5288680

period of not sleeping either properly or for long enough. Recovering from sleep restriction actually takes longer than recovery from total sleep deprivation too. Scientists now believe that there is no way of fully catching up on the physical damage to our health caused by lost sleep; it is not like a bank of tokens that can be traded on different days of the week. We can recover to the extent that we no longer feel the effects of short term sleep restriction as in tiredness but early scientific indications are that we may not ever recover from the cognitive and physical effects of longer term, poor sleep pattern. The most we can hope for is to not make it worse. Consistent sleep hygiene is an absolute self-care 'must.'

Most people need around eight hours sleep per night but some of us need more and some need less. Our individual requirements are affected by all sorts of things from genetics and age to diet and physical exertion or other health issues. The trick is to identify how much sleep our own bodies require and to do our best to make sure that happens. Signs that we have had enough sleep are obvious: if we wake feeling refreshed, we have had enough sleep. On-going tiredness or fatigue on waking means that we need more. There is an important note of caution to be added here: If we are regularly having too little sleep, we lose the ability to recognise that we are suffering from deprivation. We become accustomed to feeling the effects of lower physical, psychological and cognitive performance. Anyone who regularly sleeps for less than eight hours per night should experiment with a week's worth of a full eight hour sleeping pattern and note the effects on performance and general presentation. It may be that we had simply not realised how much stress we were applying to our bodies and minds by not allowing it the rest and recovery it needs.

The reason for feeling tired is simple: as we progress through periods of wakefulness, a chemical in the brain named adenosine (an inhibitory neurotransmitter) gradually builds up, acting as a central nervous system depressant. In normal circumstances, this build-up of adenosine promotes sleep and prevents arousal. When adenosine levels become high, we feel the need to sleep. During sleep, adenosine levels gradually fall and eventually deplete completely. It is at this point that we would wake feeling refreshed. Any residual adenosine levels in the body would leave us feeling tired.

It is for this reason that we can easily remedy the short term effects of sleep restriction or sleep debt as it is sometimes called; as we sleep more, so we give our bodies sufficient opportunity to reduce the build-up of adenosine levels and we feel less tired. If too much sleep debt accrues, that debt becomes impossible to repay. A long term restrictive sleep pattern has been linked to obesity, heart disease, cancer, Alzheimers, infertility, immune system disruption (leading to auto-immune disorders such as Multiple Sclerosis, Fibromyalgia and rheumatic issues) and diabetes as well as a shorter life expectancy.

Sleep Deprivation and Cognitive Function:

Very few of us would ever take the risk of driving a car when over the legal limit for alcohol, yet sleep deprivation affects our ability to drive safely in exactly the same way[13]. In laboratory tests, sleeping for seven hours per night rather than eight hours over ten days reduced the driver's ability to drive safely to the same level as someone who has had no sleep at all for 24 hours and the deterioration in functioning then continued to build up over time. Driving after only 15 hours without sleep reduces functioning to the same level as someone who is over the legal drink drive limit. So if we wake at 6am, by 9pm our driving ability may already be significantly impaired. This is made considerably worse if we are already sleep deprived when we wake up. Remarkably, having only 5 hours of sleep increases the risk of a car crash the following day by three times. Having four hours of sleep makes us 11.5 times more likely to have a car accident. We also know from controlled studies that combining sleep deprivation and alcohol is particularly dangerous. In a test group in the US, the group combining four hours of sleep and consuming alcohol were 30 times more likely to have an accident than those who had eight hours of sleep and no alcohol. Astonishingly, the number of vehicle accidents caused by drowsiness in the US are higher than the number caused by drugs and alcohol combined.

Reduced awareness is one factor that makes sleep deprivation so impactive upon cognitive function. Another is the complete shutdown that results from micro sleeping.

---

[13] The Royal Sociaty for the Prevention of Accidents, Driver Fatigue and Road Accidents - A Literature Review & Position Paper February 2001
https://www.rospa.com/rospaweb/docs/advice-services/road-safety/drivers/fatigue-litreview.pdf

When we are very tired, the body and mind can shut down for very short periods called micro-sleeps. This may only last for a few seconds but during that period we are unable to react to our surroundings in any way whatsoever. This is different to drink driving when reactions are often late or slow but some reaction is at least present. During a micro sleep, a driver has no control over a vehicle at all. It is clear then how dangerous this can be in a moving car. Unfortunately, there is no way to reduce the risks other than to get more sleep. The traditional methods of opening the window or singing along to loud music make no difference at all to the risk.

Only sleep will do!

Sleep Deprivation and Mental Health:

We know from our own life experiences that irritability, bad moods and a lack of focus will usually follow an occasional night with too little sleep. This is unlikely to harm our long term mental health, save in terms of functioning and memory as already described above, provided that it is not a regular occurrence. After several sleepless nights or several nights with too little sleep, the mental effects and risks become more serious. Chronic sleep debt may lead to long-term mood disorders like depression and anxiety. In a recent survey of the sleeping habits of people with anxiety or depression, most slept for less than six hours a night. Often with prolonged sleep restriction, the brain will fog, making it difficult to concentrate and make informed decisions. One of the key factors in management of mental health issues including depression and anxiety is achieving clean sleep. It genuinely is a cornerstone of wellbeing. Studies show that good sleep leads to greater physical strength but also to increased mental resilience which helps in managing every day stressors as well as significant life events. With increased resilience, we perceive ourselves to be more in control and are naturally less emotional in our reactions with better self-esteem and improved mental health.

The amygdala area of the brain dictates the extent of our emotion responses and is the switch for the 'fight or flight' sympathetic nervous system. It is kept in check by the pre-frontal cortex which promotes rational thought and decision making. After a full night's sleep, the two areas are strongly linked, enabling appropriate levels of rational control over our emotional responses. After a night of no sleep, the bond is significantly reduced, leading to a much lower ability to control our emotions. Equally, the link between the striatum and the prefrontal cortex is lessened by disturbed sleep. The striatum area of the brain controls impulsive responses and our internal rewards system. If poor sleep leaves the link between striatum and the rational thinking power of the prefrontal cortex depleted, our impulsive responses are left unchecked. This leads to risk taking and irrational or manic behaviours and 'highs' caused by the resulting dopamine release.

By switching off or diminishing the link between the 'balancing' prefrontal cortex and the emotional response centres in the brain, the result is either disproportionate highs or lows in mood or often a 'swinging' between the two. This is the same brain activity that is seen in patients diagnosed with Bi-Polar disorder.

The pattern of brain activity seen in sleep deprived subjects is remarkably similar to those identified in patients with a range of diagnosed psychiatric disorders or illness. There is no clinical evidence yet to support the suggestion that sleep deprivation causes psychiatric or psychological illness but the symptomatic presentation of brain activity and of behaviour in both circumstances is remarkably similar. It is a well and long accepted fact that disturbed sleep patterns are at least a feature of psychiatric disorders. It is true that clean sleep promotes clearer and more rational thinking which can only help a brain already struggling with the additional challenges that mental illness may bring.

Sleep Deprivation and Physical Health:

Disturbed and insufficient sleep has been indisputably linked to obesity, immune system disruption, heart disease and diabetes as well as a shorter life expectancy. Whatever the specific or individual reasons, one fact has remained true over numerous studies of millions of people: a shorter sleeping pattern will lead to a shorter life.

A lack of sleep can disrupt the immune system, leaving us less able to fend off illness and infection and increasing inflammation which in turn puts additional strain on the heart. Less sleep also causes the heart to beat more quickly and over time to calcification of the arteries, further increasing the likelihood of a heart attack. Studies have shown that people who sleep less than seven hours a day tend to gain more weight and have a higher risk of becoming obese than those who get seven or more hours of slumber[14]. During sleep, the

---

[14] 1. Patel SR, Hu FB. Short sleep duration and weight gain: a systematic review. Obesity(Silver Spring). 2008; 16:643-53.

body restores the correct levels of leptin (the chemical that makes you feel full) and ghrelin (the hunger-stimulating hormone). Without a full night's sleep, this rebalancing cannot occur and so we are left feeling unsatisfied and still hungry, even after meals. Missing out on deep sleep changes the way that the body processes glucose used by the body for energy. This can affect weight gain but again, over time, can also lead to the onset of Type 2 Diabetes. When we enter slow wave or deep sleep, nervous system activity goes down, the brain uses less glucose. Control studies have demonstrated that three nights of disrupted NREM sleep caused the subjects insulin sensitivity and glucose tolerance to reduce by 25%.[15]

During the second half of the twentieth century, obesity in the US nearly doubled. Over the same period, there was a marked reduction in average sleeping patterns. The discovery of a stark change in the body's natural ability to control appetite with hormones following sleep loss may partially explain this. Evidence suggests a possible role for chronic sleep loss in the current epidemic of obesity.

Men and women who don't get enough quality sleep have much less interest in sex and men who suffer from sleep apnoea also tend to have lower testosterone levels which can

---

2. PatelSR, Malhotra A, White DP, Gottlieb DJ, Hu FB. Association between reduced sleep and weight gain in women. Am J Epidemiol.2006; 164:947-54.

3. Taveras EM, Gilliman MW, Pena MM, Redline S, Rifas Shiman SL. Chronic Sleep Curtailment and Adiposity. Pediatrics. 2014 Jun;133(6):1013-22

[15] University of Chicago Medical Center. "Lack Of Deep Sleep May Increase Risk Of Type 2 Diabetes." ScienceDaily, 2 January 2008 www.sciencedaily.com/releases/2008/01/080101093903.htm

lower libido even further. Regular sleep disruption can impact upon fertility as the secretion of reproductive hormones is typically reduced when this occurs.

Sleep deprivation allows the sympathetic nervous system to remain activated when it should be switched off. Over time this unatural state can lead to increased blood pressure, a faltering immune system, increased swelling in the body placing additional pressure on the heart, a faster heart beat and heightened stress responses. A natural impact of insufficient sleep on the body is an increased heart rate of itself which exacerbates the pressure already felt by a cardiovascular system under strain.

A reduced sleep pattern is associated with an increase in the early evening level of the stress hormone cortisol. Normally, cortisol concentrations are falling rapidly at this time of day, heading towards minimal levels shortly before bedtime. In studies, the rate of decrease of cortisol concentrations in the early evening was approximately six times slower in subjects who had endured six days of sleep restriction than in those who had a full eight hours rest[16]. Heightened evening cortisol levels seen in chronic sleep deprivation are likely to result in insulin resistance which is a significant risk factor for obesity and diabetes.

Sleep restriction significantly impacts the thyroid axis. After six days of four-hour sleep time in studies, the normal nocturnal thyroid-stimulating hormone (TSH) level did not

---

[16] The Impact of Sleep Deprivation on Hormones and Metabolism Authors: Eve Van Cauter, PhD; Kristen Knutson, PhD; Rachel Leproult, PhD; Karine Spiegel, PhD - 2020 –
https://www.medscape.org/viewarticle/502825

rise as it should overnight, leading to TSH levels that were reduced by more than 30%. A normal pattern of TSH release reappeared when the subjects had fully recovered from the effects of reduced sleep.

During sleep, Growth hormone (GH) also called somatotropin or human growth hormone is secreted around the body by the pituitary gland. This hormone is critical to healthy growth and development as it boosts muscle mass and stimulates the growth of almost all tissues in the body including bone. Studies have demonstrated that GH secretion is altered by long term partial sleep loss.

Stimulants:

In the modern age of highly processed, high sugar content in our food and coffee additions, it is increasingly difficult to figure out when we are tired. Sugar and caffeine are both artificial stimulants that make us feel less tired than we truly are. Electronic screens have the same effect.

Caffeine works on our central nervous system in two ways: Firstly, it stops us from recognising when we are sleepy by preventing the receptors which usually sense building adenosine (the tiredness hormone that makes us feel sleepy and slows down neuro function) from working. The blocking effect means that we (a) remain awake when our body needs sleep and (b) we continue to exert our bodies and minds with a level of energy that can be damaging, given its tired state. When the blocking effect wears off, we feel a sudden tiredness descend. Every time we manage this feeling of fatigue by drinking more coffee, we make the problem much worse. Our habit loving brain soon starts sending us a message that we are in need of coffee rather than being in need of sleep!

Secondly, it acts as a stimulant on the nervous system as a whole, promoting the release of adrenalin and firing up the sympathetic nervous system. This has the same effects on the body as stress. The body's tolerance for caffeine varies from person to person and is deemed to be medically safe for most people in small doses. Indeed, some studies have also suggested that caffeine intake may protect against type 2 diabetes, Parkinson's disease, cardiovascular disease and stroke. A meta-analysis of 17 studies concluded that drinking 3–4 cups of coffee every day may increase the risk of a heart attack in men. However, in the same year, a different review of 40 studies found that drinking 2–4 cups of coffee every day had links to a reduced risk of death from all causes. It is unclear whether the caffeine in coffee is the protective element. It is likely that the caffeine is at the root of the risks.

In 1995, scientists at NASA replicated a drug study originally undertaken by a pharmacologist named Peter N Witt in 1948 and found similar results. NASA used house spiders in the study and gave them caffeine, 'speed', marijuana and amphetamines (Benzedrine). The spiders spun bizarre webs and the researchers used different statistical tools and image processors to analyse them. *"The more toxic the chemical,"* wrote the researchers in their paper, *"the more deformed a web looks in comparison with a normal web."* Clearly the effects on a spider are not identical to human responses but the webs provide a striking visual representation of the effects of these drugs on the brain's ability to function in a normal way.

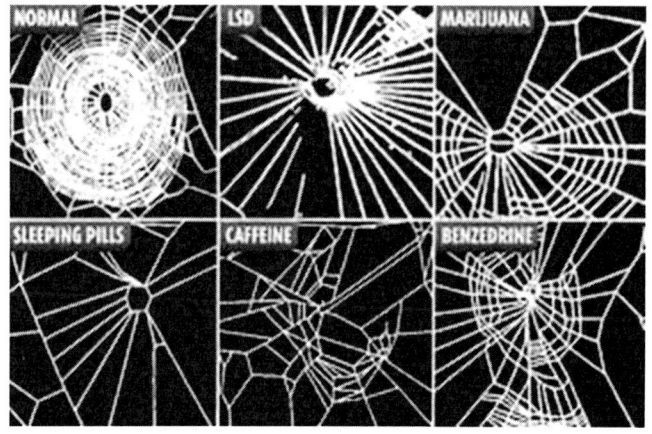

Clearly more research is necessary to establish whether long term caffeine consumption is safe and whether the benefits outweigh the risk of health problems. Certainly from a sleep-health perspective, caffeine hides the effect of sleep deprivation and therefore is best avoided, especially whilst clean sleeping habits are being established.

Sugar:

The sharp spike in our blood sugar caused by consuming sugary food and drink affects sleep in two ways. Firstly, it prevents the body from relaxing so making falling asleep more difficult. Secondly, long and short term consumption promotes inflammation in the body which has a direct effect on the quality of sleep. A 2016 study on the link between sleep and diet concluded that low fibre and high saturated fat and sugar intake is associated with lighter, less restorative sleep with more arousals. This means that sugar affects the amount of NREM sleep, critical for body and mind restoration.

Conversely, fibre has been proven to improve deep, slow-wave sleep by slowing digestion and avoiding the blood sugar spikes that accompany sweet treats. On the basis of this study, it seems that adding fibre to our evening meal and avoiding sugar is likely to help us feel full and prepare us for a good night's restorative slumber.

Screens:

The blue light emitted by screens on cell phones, computers, tablets and televisions restricts the production of melatonin, the hormone that controls our sleep / wake cycle (circadian rhythm). This makes it much harder to fall and stay asleep. Electronic devices should be avoided for an absolute minimum of 30 minutes before bedtime and kept outside of the bedroom wherever possible. If screen-time cannot be avoided then blue-light glasses may filter some but not all of the detrimental effects. Technology also keeps us awake by stimulating the mind, fooling the brain into thinking that it needs to stay awake. Late night notifications of texts, emails, calls or calendar reminders will also disturb sleep. Even if it doesn't wake us, it can prevent settled NREM sleep, thereby negatively affecting health.

The Circadian Rhythm:

The Circadian Rhythm or body clock is a theoretical master clock which coordinates the biological rhythms in a living organism. It is located in the part of the brain called the hypothalamus and receives direct input from the eyes. Signals from the environment do appear to influence circadian rhythm, specifically daylight[17]. This light can turn on or turn off genes that control the molecular structure of biological clocks. Changing the light-dark cycles can speed up, slow down or reset biological clocks as well as circadian rhythms. However, an experiment in 1968 proved that left to its own devices, the body maintains a circadian rhythm of around 24 hours even after six weeks and in complete natural darkness. Circadian rhythms can influence sleep-wake cycles, hormone release, eating habits and digestion, body temperature and other important bodily functions. It also controls the production of the sleep hormone melatonin. Irregular body clocks do exist and have been linked to various social conditions such as shift work and to chronic health conditions such as sleep disorders, obesity, diabetes, depression, bipolar disorder and seasonal affective disorder.

Shift work has been linked to an increase in the risk of a variety of physical health issues. A study in the International Journal of Cancer found a relationship between women's irregular work schedules and the rate of breast cancer being 30% higher for the women who had worked shifts[18]. Shift work has also been shown to increase the incidence of other

---

[17] Physiology, Circadian Rhythm - Sujana Reddy; Vamsi Reddy; Sandeep Sharma. July 2020.

https://www.ncbi.nlm.nih.gov/books/NBK519507/

[18] Night Shift Work and Breast Cancer Incidence: Three Prospective Studies and Meta-analysis of Published Studies - Ruth C. Travis, Angela Balkwill, Georgina K. Fensom, Paul N. Appleby, Gillian K. Reeves, Xiao-Si Wang, Andrew W. Roddam, Toral Gathani, Richard Peto, Jane Green, Timothy J. Key, and Valerie Beral - 2016 –

https://www.ncbi.nlm.nih.gov/pmc/articles/PMC5241898/

types of cancer, for example prostate cancer in men. Researchers suspect that a disruption in the circadian rhythm could pose a risk for developing the disease. Studies that manipulate the sleep / wake cycles of rodents for an extended time have resulted in faster growing tumours.

Sleep and Brain Restoration:

During sleep the brain passes through a number of 90 minute cycles of REM and NREM sleep. Each type of sleep performs a different function and has a different type of healing effect on body and mind. Whilst the cycles between REM and NREM sleep are regular; they do not contain equal amounts of REM and NREM sleep. Each cycle is different in structure. The existence of the REM / NREM 90 minute cycle ensures that even in a shorter sleep period, some of each restorative function is undertaken. However, is important to note, however, that there is more NREM and less REM sleep in the first half of the night and more REM and less NREM sleep in the latter half. The human sleep pattern leads the brain to expect to rest between 11 pm and 7 am. This means that anyone who goes to bed at 11 and only ever sleeps for 6 hours will lose between 60–90% of their REM sleep, even though they are only reducing their total sleep time by 25%. Equally, any night owl, who doesn't go to sleep until 1 am and wakes at 7 am, will lose a high proportion of NREM sleep much more than the 25% reduction in sleep time.

The Science:

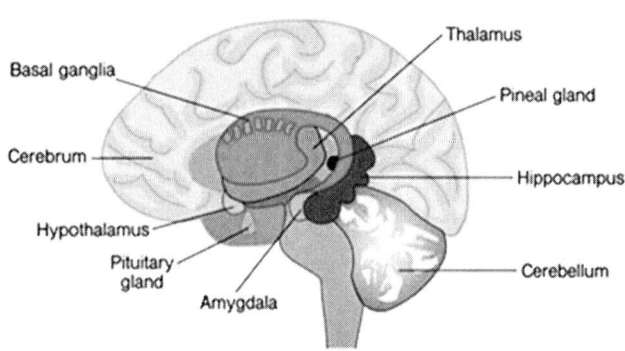

The cerebellum's job is to process procedural memories; the hippocampus is where new memories are encoded; the amygdala helps determine what memories to store and it plays a part in determining where the memories are stored based on whether we have a strong or weak emotional response to the event.

The amygdala dictates the extent of our emotion responses and is the switch for the 'fight or flight' sympathetic nervous system. The striatum lies close to the amygdala and controls deep emotional and impulsive responses and also our internal reward systems. Both the amygdala and the striatum are kept in check by the prefrontal cortex which promotes rational thought and decision making.

The hypothalamus is the memory reservoir. One of the most important functions of the hypothalamus is to link the nervous system to the endocrine system via the pituitary gland. The hypothalamus also controls body temperature, hunger, important aspects of parenting and attachment behaviours, thirst, fatigue, sleep and circadian rhythms. The posterior part of the hypothalamus is involved overall in energy balance, blood pressure, memory and learning.

The Effect of Short Sleep on the Brain:

Short terms memories (or the day's learning) are stored in an area of our brain called the hippocampus. This area of the brain acts as the memory 'reception area' where memories are stored until the brain has the chance to determine whether they require long term storage and has an opportunity to move them on. Studies have shown that brain activity during the day is high in this region when subjects are asked to recall memories from that day.

During sleep, however, the hippocampus appears to transfer the information gathered across to the cortex area of the brain. Indeed, it is the Cortex that is activated the following day in studies when the same memories are recalled. The cerebral cortex (cortex cerebri) is the outer layer of our brain that has multiple motor functions including speech and a variety of cognitive functions such as thinking and memory. This process of shifting memories from place to place takes place during the NREM phase of sleep[19]. If insufficient (or no) NREM sleep takes place then the reception area cannot clear out and will simply not allow new memories or learning in efficiently during the following day. It is for this reason that studying all night (or cramming) for

---

[19] About Sleep's Role in Memory Björn Rasch and Jan Born 2013 https://www.ncbi.nlm.nih.gov/pmc/articles/PMC3768102/

an exam is unlikely to work for long term memory recall or proper learning. The brain cannot move the new infomation into long term storage and neither can it absorb any further data. Once NREM sleep happens, the learning can move and free up space. A study at Harvard Medical School demonstrated that consolidation of learning in this way will only happen if the transfer takes place the night after the day during which the facts have been absorbed. In other words, if we don't sleep at night, we cannot be sure that anything learned during the course of that day will be properly remembered. NREM sleep functions are also disturbed if the quality of sleep is disturbed rather than sleep just being absent. It is of note that the quality of NREM sleep decreases with age, which goes some way to explaining failing memories of the ageing population.

There is now a clear and widely accepted scientific link between disruption to NREM sleep and Alzheimer's disease. The forgetfulness associated with Alzheimer's is caused by a build-up of beta-amyloid protein in certain parts of the brain. This is toxic to the neurons which surround it and so those surrounding neurons become damaged and destroyed. Amyloid protein is also present in young, healthy brains and it is the build-up rather than its presence which is damaging. The build-up of amyloid in Alzheimer's disease is in the middle part of the frontal lobe. This is not an area of the brain associated with memory but is the area of the brain responsible for generating the powerful brainwaves of deep NREM sleep - the driver of memory transfer necessary for retention. A ground breaking study by Dr Matthew Walker, PhD, (author of the remarkable book 'Why we sleep') proved the link unquestionably.

Scientists have explored the impact of sleep upon the glymphatic system in the brain. The glymphatic system uses glial cells present in the brain to absorb toxins and other harmful matter from around the brain cells and remove it as it is washed away by cerebrospinal fluid.

It was discovered that during NREM sleep, the glial cells shrank by 60%, leaving more space for the cerebrospinal fluid to wash away the debris. This enabled the glymphatic system to be 10-20% more effective than during waking hours or during other types of sleep. So without the effective brain-cleansing NREM sleep generated by the frontal lobe, amyloid build-up continues, attacking the neurons of the frontal lobe and making NREM sleep less effective. It is a self-professing, ever increasing cycle of damage. A restricted sleep pattern is therefore more likely to result in the onset of Alzheimer's and to accelerate it.

How to get better sleep:

Recovery from sleep deprivation is a lengthy process. It takes four or more full nights' sleep to restore performance after a week of short sleeping. Months of restricted sleep will result in a build-up of significant sleep debt and poor sleep hygiene habits, so recovery will take several weeks. Starting on a weekend, try to add on an extra hour or two of sleep a night. The best way to do this is to go to bed when you're tired and allow your body to wake you in the morning without an alarm. Expect to sleep for upwards of ten hours a night at first. After a while, the amount of time in sleep will gradually decrease to a normal level. Don't rely on caffeine or energy drinks as a short-term pick-me-up. They may boost energy and concentration temporarily but can disrupt sleep patterns even further in the long term.

Of course, it is always better to identify the root cause of any chronic problem and deal with it properly for a long term fix. This is likely to involve a process of elimination as physical and emotional or psychological causes are discounted.

As with a baby, a regular bedtime routine will help the mind and body prepare for sleep. Commitment to this health goal is important to achieve results as it would be to a new eating or exercise regime. All stimulants should be avoided including sugar, caffeine, electronic screens or bright light for as long as possible before bedtime. If possible, caffeine should be avoided altogether (keep in mind that caffeine withdrawal will come with its own side effects including headaches and restless sleep). Limiting fluids at least one hour before bedtime will help reduce the chances of being woken to use the toilet. Bear in mind that if inflammation is an issue, fluid release is likely to commence once the body is in a restful state and so this may require additional toilet breaks during the night, too. This should subside as a new self-care regime becomes established. Relaxing activities before bedtime will help, including sleep tea, reading (not on a screen!), bathing, especially using herbal remedies such as lavender or epsom salts. A Himalayan Rock Salt lamp will create a calm and serene atmosphere and promote relaxation.

If falling asleep is an issue, distraction can help either with meditation or music, specifically designed to slow the rhythm of the body and promote restful sleep. A sleep story can also sometimes distract from the worry of not being able to sleep in a pattern of chronic sleep deprivation, helping the body and mind to relax enough to finally rest. There are a variety of free tools available online.

> MANTRA for restful sleep: I choose to rest my body and mind, to recuperate and restore.

Exercise: Keep a sleep diary for two weeks. Write in it how much water, sugar, alcohol and caffeine you consume throughout the day, noting the time. Note the time of your meals and the kind of foods that you ate. Write down what you had been doing (generally) during the day and in particular, what your bedtime routine was that evening and how you felt. Note the time that you went to bed and in the morning, record what time you most likely went to sleep, whether you had wandering thoughts and how long you slept for. Make a record of how you feel, refreshed or otherwise. After two weeks, review your diary and look for patterns. (Note: Menstruating ladies, you may want to continue for a full month or two as menstruation can affect sleep cycles). See what links you can identify between behaviour, mood, food and fluid intake and the quality or length of sleep that you have.

Reflection: Think about a worry that you have that can race through your thoughts when trying to sleep. What is at the root of that worry? Is there a fear associated with it? What is it that you are worried about? Byron Katie, creator of the self-betterment process 'The Work', suggests asking four simple questions for help, bring worry into focus and perspective. and are designed to help you address your worries head-on:

1. Is your worry true? (Yes or no. If no, move to three)
2. Can you absolutely know that it's true? (Yes or no.)
3. How do you react and what happens to your body and mind when you believe that thought?
4. Who would you be without the thought?

In undertaking this process, we can identify when we are worrying about things that may not even be true and how our worrying is harming us. Once we have established that, it becomes easier to bring the worry into sharper focus and consider whether it is something that we should be spending time thinking about. Coupled with a practise of mindfulness, we can begin to let these things pass through our mind unless we have specifically and consciously decided to allow them some headspace. We begin to take control of our thinking and therefore our worrying, a key component of restful sleep.

Chapter 10
Fuel

Food can either make you sick or make you well. It is the fuel that drives your body. The quality of what you put in will determine how well your body and mind operate and for how long optimum performance can be sustained. Everyone knows that eating food that is 'off' can make us sick within minutes but few of us truly appreciate that eating food that the body was not designed to consume can make us sick little by little over years and years. Our digestive system drives so many aspects of our biology that keep us healthy over time. It houses 80% of our immune system and so it stands to reason that the two are intrinsically linked. If we pour anything except the best fuel into our vehicles, we cannot expect to get the best out of it. It is no coincidence that the World Cancer Research Fund has made evidence based links between health and food, for example, estimating that 45% of bowel cancer could be prevented through diet, physical activity and weight management.[20]

---

[20] Diet, Nutrition, Physical Activity and Cancer: a Global Perspective. Continuous Update Project Expert Report 2018. Available at dietandcancerreport.org

We have all been subjected to a barrage of conflicting information over the years about 'healthy eating', from the low fat diets of the 80s and the low sugar, high saccharine diets of the 90s, through Atkins and Dukan to Paleo, the baby food diet and, perhaps, the least appealing, the cabbage soup diet! Each fad promised its loyal following a slender waist in record time but was ultimately replaced as being unsustainable or unhealthy in some other respect and so was dispensed with. Cue the arrival of the next 'miracle' weight loss solution…and so the cycle continued and the pounds went back on. In reality, there is no substitute for establishing good, clean, healthy eating patterns. Established habits are much more likely to endure and bring about long lasting and more meaningful benefits for maintenance of healthy weight loss and general wellbeing. Reducing our intake of sugar, gluten, processed foods and alcohol are great places to start. Little indulgences won't hurt and won't tip the balance into poor digestive health as long as they are controlled and infrequent. Clean, healthy and balanced everyday eating lets us savour the treats with guilt-free pleasure!

There is no right or wrong 'diet' for society. When it comes to identifying which foods are well tolerated and not so well tolerated by our own body, our stomachs are the very best indicators. The gut is a great communicator known in science as the second brain. The obvious indicator of what is suiting us as individuals is if a food makes you feel bloated, uncomfortable or gassy. If we are to develop good digestive health, we must learn to listen to our gut; very often it' knows better than our brain! Our digestive system is the very foundation of our health in ways much more complex than most people realise…The gastrointestinal tract is key to human good health; It transports food from the mouth to the stomach, turns it into absorbable nutrients and stored energy and shifts waste back out of the body. As we learn to think about the body and mind as one moving part it follows that if you don't properly nourish yourself, you don't live well.

It's really that simple.

In recent years, scientists have discovered that the digestive system has an even bigger, more complex job than previously appreciated. It's been linked to numerous aspects of health that have seemingly nothing to do with digestion from immunity to emotional stress to chronic illnesses including cancer and Type 2 diabetes. Science has demonstrated that the digestive tract is full of trillions of bacteria (known as the Micro-biome) that not only help us process food but that also help our bodies maintain balance and overall well-being. Research on the micro-biome is still in its infancy but studies have already found that certain environments, foods and behaviours can influence gut health for better or worse. The microbes in our gut (or gut flora) feed on the food that we put into our gut and multiply accordingly. Once established, if we don't feed the existing flora the food it craves, it will send messages to our brain to tell us that we need it; cravings. Different flora feed on different foods and so the more sugary food we eat, the more we encourage multiplication of the flora that crave sugar. If we starve the gut flora associated with sugar, the numbers reduce leaving space for flora which requires more nutritious food stuffs.

In turn and to truly appreciate the benefits that proper nutrition can have upon our wellbeing is important to recognise the impact that gut health can have on our physical and emotional behaviour as well as the other way around.

Technically known as the enteric nervous system or the 'second brain' as scientists have labelled it, our digestive system consists of sheaths of neurons embedded in the nine-metre long walls of the long tube of our gut. The second brain contains a remarkable 100 million neurons which is more than in the spinal cord or even in the central nervous system.

The multitude of neurons in the enteric nervous system (digestive system) enables us to 'feel' the inner world of our gut and its contents, leaving the highly complex business of digestion to the second brain without troubling the brain in the head. Much of this second brain firepower is used in the elaborate daily grind of digestion but research has shown that the gut's complexity probably cannot be interpreted through this process alone. The unique and remarkable vagus nerve constantly carries information between our stomach and our brain, an astonishing 80–90% of which is carried from the gut to the brain and not the other way around. This means that our gut sends many, many more messages to the brain than the brain sends to the gut.

The second brain informs our state of mind in other more obscure ways as well. A significant proportion of our emotional responses are probably influenced by the nerves in our gut. Butterflies in the stomach when excited, feelings of nausea when nervous and disturbed digestive function or absence of hunger when stressed are examples of signalling from the gut to the brain as part of our physiological response to our environment. It also explains the concept of comfort eating and the link between some psychological disorders and food, such as bulimia or anorexia. Emerging science suggests that everyday emotional well-being may rely on messages from the brain in the gut to the brain in our heads more than we have previously realised too. For example, electrical stimulation of the vagus nerve, which carries messages between brain and tummy, is used as a beneficial treatment for depression, indicating to maintain balanced or positive mood; our vagus nerve must be functioning well to efficiently carry messages between gut and brain.

As science embraces the notion that our bodies and psychology are closely enmeshed, the field of neuro-gastroenterology will offer new insight into the workings of the second brain and its impact on the body and mind. Studies are beginning to systematically consider connections between diseases and lesions in the gut's nervous system and research is currently investigating how the second brain mediates the body's immune response through management of inflammation and the expulsion of foreign invaders. This connection has huge implications for prevention and management of immunodeficiency and related disorders such as rheumatoid arthritis, fibromyalgia, MS and psoriasis to name but a few.

Our bodies are precious. They are the vessel in which we live, breath, laugh and love. They are designed to be miraculous healing machines but they are limited in how efficiently they can continue to work if they are not nurtured. The body was never designed to break down sugary, dense, complex, artificial or processed substances that make up much of the convenience 'food' that we eat these days. It is stressful for the body to process. It often contains chemicals which are permitted in food in small doses but which the body finds extremely difficult to expel. This means that they build up, as does the damage that these chemicals and sugar cause.

We get one shot at taking care of our precious bodies. Grab it with both hands!

Sugar:

Cut out sugar as much as possible from the diet. Sugar is in many of our foods but often disguised in the labelling under one of its aliases. There are at least 61 different names for sugar listed on food labels. These include common names such as sucrose and high-fructose corn syrup, galactose, glucose, fructose, lactose, maltose as well as barley malt, dextrose, sucrose and rice syrup among others. Sugar has a multitude of hidden side effects on the body. From the known impacts on the liver, on neurotransmitter dysregulation, stimulating inflammation and increasing cellular ageing. We are also learning more from ever emerging science that sugar is related to a significant increase in cancer risk. Researchers at The University of Texas: MD Anderson Cancer Centre found that:

"Sucrose intake in mice comparable to levels of Western diets led to increased tumour growth and metastasis when compared to a non-sugar starch diet," Dr Peiying Yang, a co-author of the study.

There has never been a better time to get rid of this wellbeing drain from the diet. Be aware of hidden sugar in foods like ready-made sauces, fruit juices and breakfast cereal. Definitely don't add sugar to anything. It will take a couple of weeks to truly wean yourself from your sugar addiction which most of us unwittingly suffer but it will be worth it.

Eating sugary foods regularly actually changes the taste buds so that they no longer sense sweetness in the same way and can eventually be damaged from eating too much. An American study has provided empirical evidence that changes in consumption of simple sugars influence the perception of sweet taste intensity. The gut also has receptors which 'taste' fats and sugars. These receptors influence the release of hormones that control blood sugar, hunger and appetite. Leptin is the hormone that helps regulate our appetite and makes our bodies less sensitive to sweet taste. Anyone with obesity has a very high level of leptin and so has to have much more sweetness to taste it. Losing weight and reducing BMI levels (and so reducing leptin levels) can help increase sensitivity to sweetness and reduce sugar cravings.

When we consume sugar, the body experiences a 'high' followed by a 'crash' which results in us feeling hungry or craving more sugar. The high we experience is caused by the release in the brain of opioids and dopamine. This response is part of the brain's 'rewards' system and causes addiction to the feeling of the dopamine release. We the associate the sugar with the dopamine feeling we crave and so we become addicted to the sugar. This is the same associative process that leads to addictions to all sorts of things, from social media to alcohol. A diet containing a high sugar level along with many other processed and chemical 'foods' can actually damage the protective gut lining, allowing harmful microbes to attack your stomach and intestinal tissue. This can lead to inflammation and infection as well as more long-term chronic disease. Make no mistake, cutting out sugar is much more difficult than it sounds, laregly because it is often so well hidden by the manufacturers, but is so very important to overall health and wellbeing. The whole body will adjust to a lower baseline level of sugar stimulation in just a few weeks. Taste buds come alive again, weight reduces and healthiness soars. It is a challenge well worth the effort. After a while, your body will rid itself of the cravings and stop telling you that your new, more healthy eating plan is boring and tasteless. Your taste buds will wake up to the new flavours in your food and help you get back to enjoying nature's produce at its best.

Processed food:

Say a firm and consistent NO to processed foods. Processed foods aren't just microwave meals and other ready meals. A processed food is any food that has been altered some way during its preparation before it reaches your home and can be mechanically processed or chemically processed. Not all processing is bad for us; pasteurising milk (if you eat dairy produce) is one obvious example, although there are benefits in consuming unpasteurised produce too. Processing provides the opportunity for manufacturers to add sugar, salt and chemical additives to foods whilst removing some of its nutritional content. This makes it longer lasting and more flavourful for the consumer but also often make it harder for our bodies to break down. Ultra processed food consumption has now been positively linked to an increased cancer risk. Processing loads our food with unnatural and unnecessary sugar, sodium and fat and is designed to make you addicted to them so that you overeat them and then buy more. Fizzy pop is a manufacturers dream!

Processed foods also usually contain a plethora of artificial ingredients which we don't understand. In short, processed foods are linked by scientific research to a multitude of health problems such as heart disease, obesity, diabetes and changes in behaviour. It is odd then that we continue to consume so much of it, especially when more nutritious, fresh food tastes so good on its own. Making time to eat well can be a challenge so setting boundaries for our consumption in advance and food planning can help so much. Our food is not a toy so why would we take the risk of eating it after someone has played around with it? If we don't know what our food contains, should we be consuming it? An important part of the wellbeing agenda is becoming aware and accepting that everything we do to, with and for ourselves is our own choice. If someone gave us a pill and told us to take it without any other information, we would refuse. So why do we take the same risks with our food, just because it's in a shape or form that we recognise? Be aware of nutritional information but also take care to read the ingredients list. If we see something we don't understand on the list we should put it back, at least until we do know and can make a concsious choice about whether we want to consume it or not! Taking control of our nutritional health will provide a sense of accountability for what we consume, benefiting our mental as well as our physical health.

Probiotics:

Probiotics are the good bacteria that our gut needs to stay healthy and bio-diverse and prebiotics provide fuel for the good probiotic bacteria. If probiotics were the seeds in a garden, prebiotics would be the water and the sunshine. They work in sync with each other, so our digestive system needs both to maintain good gastro health. Live yoghurt is an excellent source of so-called friendly probiotic bacteria. Kefir is a probiotic yoghurt drink made by fermenting milk and is packed with good bacteria. Non-dairy alternatives include miso, sauerkraut, kimchi, kombucha, pickles, sourdough, almonds and olive oil. If those foods will feel difficult to add into the diet, a Probiotics supplement can supply live colonies of beneficial bacteria that aid digestion and eliminate harmful bacteria and toxins in the gut. When choosing a probiotic, look for the term 'billions of live cultures' instead of 'millions of live cultures'. Although both terms seem to be broadly the same, millions of cultures do not usually provide enough benefit to the digestive system. It is important to make sure that the way the supplement is delivered will not cause it to be destroyed by the gut and that its valuable contents will make it as far as the colon! The most common probiotics are a part of the Lactobacillus and Bifido-bacterium families because they are deemed safe and generally have no side effects. Apple cider vinegar (choose the option 'with the mother') contains antimicrobial, antifungal and antiviral properties as well as probiotics and prebiotics that repair your gastrointestinal system and keep it healthy.

Prebiotics:

Prebiotics are a type of dietary fibre that remains intact as it passes through the gut and then lower intestine. There it helps to promote probiotics or good bacteria that our gut needs to function efficiently. Prebiotics can be found in Raw Chicory Root, Raw Jerusalem Artichoke, Raw Dandelion Greens, Raw Garlic, Raw Leeks, Raw Onion, Cooked Onions, Asparagus, Chickpeas, lentils, red kidney beans, baked beans, soybeans, cashews, pistachio, nuts and bananas. A supplement can also be useful to boost prebiotic levels in the gut. Boosting prebiotics feeds the naturally present bifidobacteria, encouraging it to fight harmful bacteria in the intestines, prevent constipation and give the immune system a boost. Furthermore, evidence indicates that bifidobacteria helps to reduce intestinal concentrations of certain carcinogenic enzymes which may cause cancer. Increasing prebiotic fibre intake also supports immunity, generally digestive health, bone density, bowel efficiency, weight management and brain health.

Food as medicine:

For thousands of years in Eastern medicine, the produce of nature has been used to heal the body. It is only relatively recently in the last 100 years or so that the western world has diverted its faith in nature to faith in the more modern, scientific approach of using synthetic chemical alternatives. Any breakthrough in medicine is, of course, to be received with gratitude but that doesn't mean that we should leave behind the wisdom of the ancient Traditional Eastern

Medicinal practitioners, philosophies or the 'old wives tales' that helped keep our ancestors well.

Old wives tales are generally not fanciful. Usually they are based upon a genuine property or remedy which gives the body a genuine boost. For example, the old adage that carrots hep you to see in the dark is true! Carrots contain vitamin A or retinol and this is required for your body to synthesise rhodopsin, which is the pigment in your eyes that operates in low-light conditions. If you have a vitamin A deficiency, you will develop nyctalopia or night blindness. The science provides the answer to the mystery!

Plants often have untapped healing properties that can be used cheaply and effectively to treat all sorts of maladies. Their easy accessibility can provide immediate relief whilst waiting for western medical treatment or provide an alternative remedy. A good example of this is the anti-inflammatory properties of the weeds we find in our own gardens like the nettle leaf or dandelion. Studies show the nettle leaf to be as effective as many anti-inflammatory drugs, especially for arthritis, joint and muscle pain. It gently stimulates the lymphatic system, releasing toxic waste through the kidneys. It is rich in iron, excellent for circulation, red blood cells, anaemia and fatigue. It is similar to dandelion leaf in eliminating uric acid from joints. Nettle leaves can be steamed like spinach served with butter (they won't sting your mouth) or to make a mild refreshing tea that can be sweetened with honey. The humble dandelion is equally remarkable. The leaves, flowers and buds can all be eaten raw in salads. Dandelion helps the liver and gall bladder break down fat for detoxification and the kidneys as a diuretic. They have a taste similar to chicory and are packed full of vitamins and minerals. Dandelion leaves provide potassium, magnesium, niacin, calcium, phosphorus, proteins, iron, sulphur, zinc, vitamins B1, B2, B6, B12, C and E. These compounds regulate fluid balance and balance nerve and muscle signals, reduce blood pressure, adjust blood glucose levels, regulate immune function, improve learning and memory and much more.

The 'Aromatherapy Nature's Way' website is an amazing encyclopaedia of knowledge based on clinical studies and trials. Speaking about her experience of the use of citrus oils in healing, American physician Dr Veronique Desaulniers, well-known for her unique approach to health and wellness during her 30 years of practice and an early professional advocate of essential oils in American healthcare states that "citrus oils are breast cancer busters. One type of oil that stands out when it comes to its effect on breast cancer is limonene, an extract of citrus peels, some spices and herbs." She notes that "there are many studies that have shown limonene to have many anticancer benefits. There are decades of animal research as well as human research, which explain the mechanism of how this essential oil affects the body. The evidence is compelling enough for WebMD.com to state that it is used to prevent and treat cancer. Specifically for breast cancer, limonene activates Phase II detoxification of the liver which results in neutralising cancer-causing chemicals that kill off cancer cells. After ingesting 2 grams of limonene per day for six weeks before surgery, scientists found high concentrations of limonene in the breast tissue as well as reduced tumour growth. In fact, limonene has been shown to inhibit or prevent breast cancer development.[21]" A 2017 study also discovered that limonene epoxide helps to prevent inflammation.

These are just a few of the remarkable benefits that nature's medicine cupboard can provide. Whatever the condition, the natural world will have created something to help. It is not suggested that these will work better or should be taken in preference to clinical solutions. It is clear from research that the benefits of plants as medicine can easily be incorporated into a supplemental regime or even better still, incorporated into our diet through careful research and making different choices. Most are readily available and again come with the additional and extremely important benefit of making us feel that we are taking back some control over the ailments that trouble us.

Antibiotics:

It is a little known fact that a course of antibiotics will kill the good bacteria in our gut as well as the bad bacteria it was prescribed to deal with. This means that after a course of antibiotics, it is imperative to focus on restoring the gut flora and microbiome. Failure to do so can leave our already tired immune systems weak and more susceptible to further infection and illness. Strengthening the immune system and maintaining it robustly will provide a truly solid foundation for good physical and mental health.

---

[21] https://www.aromatherapynaturesway.com/aromatherapy-science/

Hormones in food:

For many years, young cattle were injected with hormones to help them grow more quickly and gain more weight and also increase milk production in order to increase profitability for farmers. Synthetic oestrogen and testosterone were the most common hormones used. There are no independent studies indicating the safety of such farming methods for humans and so responding to the lack of certainty, the European Union banned all hormones in beef. Japan, Canada, Australia, New Zealand and the EU have banned rBGH which stimulates milk production in dairy cattle. The fact remains that hormones are naturally present in milk, whether processed with added synthetic hormones or otherwise.

Whilst no industry funded studies have demonstrated a link between dairy consumption and a risk to human health, an independent study in 2015 which also combined and analysed date from other available studies concluded that "the collected data from other researchers and our own data are indicating that the presence of steroid hormones in dairy products could be counted as an important risk factor for various cancers in humans".[22]

It has long been known and medically accepted that the risk of breast cancer may be increased with higher lifetime exposure to oestrogen. Indeed, the amount of hormone that enters a person's bloodstream even after eating hormone-treated meat is small compared with the amount of oestrogen

---

[22] Malekinejad, Hassan; Rezabakhsh, Aysa - 2015 - Hormones in Dairy Foods and Their Impact on Public Health - A Narrative Review Article, Iranian journal of public health

our bodies produces daily. However, even low levels changes in hormones can have strong effects on some body processes. Some scientists have suggested that the increase in hormone consumption could be causing or exacerbating the trend towards earlier puberty, although this is difficult to measure as hormones are produced in the body as well as consumed.

Plastic consumption:

An American study published in 'Environmental Science and Technology[23]' took data from 26 previous studies that measured the amount of microplastic particles in food and air based on average lifestyle factors. They concluded that yearly microplastics consumption ranges between 39000 and 52000 particles in food alone, depending upon age and sex. These estimates increase to 74000 and 121000 when inhalation from the air is considered. Additionally, anyone who meets their recommended water intake through only bottled sources may be consuming an additional 90000 microplastic particles per year compared to 4000 for those who drink only tap water. These estimates are subject to large amounts of variation but are likely underestimates. The European commission's chief scientific advisers said in a report in April 2019 that "the evidence [on the environmental and health risks of microplastics] provides grounds for genuine concern and for precaution to be exercised".

---

[23] Human Consumption of Microplastics, Kieran D. Cox*, Garth A. Covernton, Hailey L. Davies, John F. Dower, Francis Juanes, and Sarah E. Dudas - Environ. Sci. Technol. 2019, 53, 12, 7068–7074

Chemicals in daily life:

"Modern production of foods incorporates a wide range of synthetic chemicals," says Jeff Gillman, PhD, associate professor of horticulture at the University of Minnesota. *"Many of these chemicals have the potential to be very damaging to humans if they are exposed to high concentrations, or to low concentrations over an extended period of time."* Craig Minowa, American environmental scientist with the Organic Consumers Association, a non-profit advocacy group, has said, *"More people are realising there's a myriad of chemicals in conventionally produced food,"* noting that *"most of the studies on safety are done or supported by the [manufacturing] companies themselves"*. It is worth also remembering that the safe levels of chemicals in consumption are sometimes exceeded over time if residue remains in the body. This is not usually tested as part of safety studies, especially those that are manufacturer -led.

It is unavoidable that some of the chemicals used in the chemical processes in food production will be released into the environment or left on or in the products that we buy. As a result, they can end up in our food, water, air and homes and ultimately are consumed into our bodies. Most of us are unaware of these chemicals, even though they can affect our health and wellbeing. As we go about our daily business, we constantly come in to contact with chemicals. These may be in the cleaning products we use in our homes and on ourselves and in our hair, chlorine in swimming pools, pesticides on food, toxic plastic and foam components in our household furniture, food storage containers and wrapping and in our water supply.

Whilst we are unlikely to be able to avoid them completely, an awareness of what is contained in or left on the products we bring into our homes will help us to reduce them. Some chemicals still used in shampoos and personal hygiene products, for example, fragrance enhancer diethyl phthalate, the preservative benzyl benzoate, the synthetic fragrance galaxolide and heavy metals can cause skin irritation and endocrine disruption. We would never imagine that 'brain fog' or bloating could be caused by our deodorant but it is technically possible, especially if the effects have been able to build up over a long period of time!

Opting for the most natural products using the most natural ingredients and prepared with minimal processing offers the best chance of avoiding anything that may cause us harm or knock our natural balance out of line. Increased awareness at least allows us to each make our own choices about what, if any, risks we are prepared to take with our own health or the health of our families. It is also important to buy organic where possible and affordable and to wash fresh fruit and vegetables thoroughly before eating to get rid of any 'tolerance' (permitted) level pesticides left on foodstuffs. Soaking in baking soda and water has been shown to be a more effective way of removing chemicals than bleach (which, of course, should not be consumed).

Meat:

There has been much publicity around the benefits of vegetarian and vegan diets. There are, as always, pros and cons to each. The moral and ethical arguments for and against meat consumption continue to rage, the middle ground being ethical production. The rights and wrongs of consumption of animal produce are not the focus of this book, only some of the nutritional benefits and disadvantages are dealt with here.

Traditionally, meat has been a significant part of the western diet. While data from Defra's Family Food report[24] shows there has been little change in the proportion of meat people were buying in the UK between 1974 and 2011; there was a marked difference in the type of meat being purchased. Ready meals and convenience meat products (usually processed) had seen a steady increase, white meat a modest increase (overtaking red meat for the first time in 1988) whilst the sales of red meat have steadily declined. Sales of red meat have sharply fallen over more recent years.

Meat is a good source of protein, vitamins and minerals in the diet. In 2016, Public Health England's new dietary advice recommended people halve their dairy intake and eat less meat, replacing it with beans and pulses in which similar nutritional elements can also be found. The Department of Health advised in 2016 that the average adult daily consumption in the UK should be no more than 70g (a McDonalds beef patty weighs 45g). Vegan activists claim that this was in response to the huge body of scientific evidence showing how harmful meat and dairy are to health. Indeed, it is right to say that affect upon the human body of hormones and antibiotics historically present in animal feed and may therefore be transferred into our food chain remains unknown.

---

[24] Defra Family Food Report 2015 –
https://assets.publishing.service.gov.uk/government/uploads/system/uploads/attachment_data/file/485982/familyfood-2014report-17dec15.pdf

We do know that around 75% of the world's soy production is destined for animal feed and that soy contains phytoestrogens or plant-based oestrogen that behaves like oestrogen, the female sex hormone, within the body. Whether they are added synthetically or otherwise, generated through animal feed or medical administration, hormones and chemicals that interfere with our endocrine systems are naturally present in animal products and anyone trying to control their consumption of hormones or antibiotics may therefore wish to limit their intake of animal produce generally.

The nutritional value of processed meat is depleted. Processed meat includes any meat that is preserved by smoking, curing, salting or adding preservatives. Bacon, sausages, salami, ham and pâtés are all examples of processed meats. These foods are often high in both saturated fat and salt and provide much less than unprocessed meat in the way of vitamins and minerals.

Beans, peas and lentils (types of pulses or legumes) are good nutritional alternatives to meat because they're naturally very low in fat and they're high in fibre, protein, vitamins and minerals. Pulses are edible seeds that grow in pods and include foods like lentils, chickpeas, beans and peas. Other vegetable-based sources of protein include tofu, bean curd and mycoprotein (a highly processed product, produced by means of a fermentation process, which starts off with a natural type of fungus, Fusarium venenatum – not licensed as food in Canada). All of these products are now widely available in most retailers.

Soya:

A World Wildlife Fund report in 2014 concluded that the vast majority of the world's soya – around 75% – is destined for the production of protein-rich animal feed for livestock, especially poultry and pigs. World demand for soya-based feed has dramatically increased in line with world demand. Regrettably, this has sometimes been at the expense of some of the world's most vital forests, grasslands and savannahs being cleared for soya fields. The WWF estimated in 2014 that approximately 80% of the world's soya is now genetically modified. More than 93% of the corn and soy planted in the United States is genetically modified in some way.

Soy was historically genetically modified to improve the quality of soy oil. Soy oil has a fatty acid profile that makes it susceptible to oxidation. This makes it quickly go rancid and it is therefore of limited usefulness to the food industry. Genetic modification offered greater possibilities for increased shelf life and profitability, to grow more soy at a minimal cost to meet the rapidly escalating demand and to reduce the impact of glyphosate (a toxic chemical used as a weed killer and also known as Round Up) on the crop. GM producers claim that the GM processing offers advantages and added value for the consumer including improved nutritional composition or even therapeutic effects.

The nutritional benefits of whole soy foods including soy beans, edamame, tofu, tempeh and soy milk are considerable; they contain a variety of phytochemicals and antioxidants that work to protect against heart disease, some cancers and type 2 diabetes. Soy is also high in protein and fibre, has a variety of both vitamins and minerals, contains healthy fats and is relatively low in calories. The risk factors with soy include phytoestrogens or plant based oestrogens and an unknown impact from any genetic modification. These potential endocrine disruptors consist mainly of two isoflavones, genistein and daidzein, that act like the female sex hormone oestrogen within the body. Because oestrogen plays a role in everything from some breast cancers to sexual reproduction, this is where most of the soy controversy originates. More research is needed to identify whether the soy derivative binds to the oestrogen receptors and reduces the amount of binding that hormonal oestrogen is able to do and whether this process, if indeed it does occur, is damaging or helpful for the body. Each individual will, therefore, need to weigh the benefits against the risk of soy consumption in whatever its form, carefully considering what they hope to achieve from their diet. As always, awareness of what we are consuming and how our diet is likely to impact upon our mind and body is key.

Carbs:

Carbohydrate foods generally contain three elements; starch, sugar and fibre. All nutritional researchers agree that dietary fibre is an essential element of the diet, assisting with digestive health and regular bowel movements. Fibre also helps you feel fuller for longer, improving cholesterol and blood sugar levels and can assist in preventing some diseases such as diabetes, heart disease and bowel cancer. Starch is found in foods that come from plants. Starchy foods such as bread, rice, potatoes and pasta provide a slow and steady release of energy throughout the day. A fibre rich diet will also help to encourage good bacteria in the gut (pre and probiotics).

Starchy foods can be a valuable source of energy. However, once inside the digestive system, they are broken down into glucose which is sugar. This energy source is then processed by the body in the same way as sugar is. It is important to note that some starchy foods can provide important nutrients to the diet including B vitamins, iron, calcium and folate and may also provide fibre.

Bread is now available in a plethora of shapes colours and sizes. Wholemeal is the most nutritious as it contains the whole wheat kernel and fibre-rich bran offering twice as much iron, three times as much zinc and four times as much fibre as basic white bread. It provides B group vitamins (thiamine and niacin), Vitamin E, iron, selenium and other minerals, phytonutrients and bran, a useful source of fibre. Milling wheat into white flour removes the outer bran coat and wheat-germ, losing most of the thiamine, niacin and iron in the process. During the Second World War, calcium carbonate (E170) was added to white and brown flours to add dietary calcium. Since 1997, UK produced white flour is no longer allowed to be bleached but bread manufactured using flour produced in other countries may be. Some loaves have soya flour added to make them more white in colour. Brown bread lovers have to be avid label readers to know what they are getting from their loaf! Sometimes brown bread is made from wholemeal flour but sometimes it is made from white milled flour and has caramel added to change the colour. Again, awareness is the key to making informed choices here.

Sugars are also a type of carbohydrate. The type of sugars that most adults and children in the UK eat too much of are called free sugars. These are sugars that are added to food or drinks such as biscuits, chocolate, flavoured yoghurts, breakfast cereals and fizzy drinks. The sugars in honey, syrups (such as maple, agave and golden syrup), nectars (such as blossom) and unsweetened fruit juices, vegetable juices and smoothies are more naturally occurring sugars but these still count as free sugars. They are classed as carbohydrates because they provide the body with energy. However, the effect of sugar on the body is known to be damaging, whether from a natural or processed source. Researchers at The University of Texas: MD Anderson Cancer Centre gave groups of mice four different diets and found that at six-months-old rodents eating the largest amount of sucrose were more susceptible to cancerous lumps on their mammary glands. A remarkable 60% of mice on sucrose-enriched diets developed the tumours according to the study published in the Cancer Research journal. Less than a third of the mice on starch-controlled diets had breast cancer, researchers noted. Dr Peiying Yang, a co-author of the study noted that the findings were clear, stating, "We found that sucrose intake in mice comparable to levels of Western diets led to increased tumour growth and metastasis when compared to a non-sugar starch diet."

Foods which contain fibre and yet are low starch include Flax seeds, Chia seeds, Avocado, Almonds, Unsweetened coconut meat, Blackberries, Raspberries, Pistachios, Cauliflower, Broccoli, Wheat bran, Aubergine, Asparagus and Red / Purple cabbage. Wheat bran is the hard outer coating of the wheat kernel. While it's found naturally in whole grains, it can also be purchased on its own to add texture and a nutty flavour to foods like baked goods, smoothies, yogurt, soups and casseroles. It is rich in several important vitamins and minerals including selenium and manganese. It also contains a good amount of insoluble fibre to help treat constipation and promote regular bowel movements.

A note of caution in respect of any non-organic cereal and grain is that they may be harvested with glyphosate. This category includes wheat, barley, buckwheat, millet, rice, oats, wild rice, popcorn and sorghum and also the major GM foods such as soy, corn, and canola. The difficulty with these kinds of products if buying them already processed (in cereal for example) is that it is impossible to wash them thoroughly to ensure that no chemicals remain. All foodstuffs have a permitted 'tolerance' level for chemicals used in farming and production and it is impossible to understand the impact on the body of a build-up of such toxins over time or indeed the effect of the chemicals when combined with others. As always, home grown is best, closely followed by organic farming methods if they are available and affordable.

Alcohol:

As well as usually containing a great deal of sugar, alcoholic drinks contain a high number of calories which can impact upon weight. Fat, especially on men tends to go to the belly and belly fat is more dangerous than other fats. Eventually it squeezes the organs and can also release harmful chemicals into the blood, increasing the risk of heart disease, diabetes and even dementia. Too much alcohol can change the brain's ability to stay balanced and run smoothly. The more we drink, the more our brains are affected, making us nervous and in low mood. Our judgment, including our ability to keep ourselves safe is impaired. Alcohol can also further impact upon proper sleep, leaving us even more sluggish and irritable. Regularly having even just a couple of pints of lager can weaken the heart and shrink the arteries. This makes it harder for blood to be pumped and pass through, which increases blood pressure. That same pressure can lead to blood clots which can cause strokes and brain damage.

Alcohol is a poison. The liver is charged with breaking down the chemicals in the body and when it has to deal with too much alcohol, it can struggle to do its job and can become fatty and scarred. Alcohol can negatively affect the gut too. It can cause the stomach acid that is designed to break down food to attack the lining of the stomach and the muscles that surround it instead. Alcohol is high in calories and carbs, so when these are washed down into the gut, they put it under strain. That's why we can feel bloated after consuming alcohol as our intestines try to manage the additional load. Regularly drinking too much alcohol can cause more severe effects like nausea, vomiting, ulcers and even stomach cancer if left untreated. Alcohol also slows and prevents the release of sex hormones in men, affecting blood flow to the penis and this can make it harder to get and sustain an erection. Moreover, alcohol can damage the testicles over time and this can also lower testosterone levels and harm fertility.

Supplements:

A diet rich in a variety of fresh food should be sufficient to maintain good health, however, sometimes we may need an extra boost. Often the modern diet is heavy in nutrient – poor processed foods, refined grains and added sugars which are all linked to inflammation and chronic disease. Ageing, food processing and over farming (including depleted soil quality) may all contribute to poorer nutritional input. As we get older, our ability to absorb nutrients from food decreases. Also, our energy needs aren't the same and we tend to eat less.

A 2015 study by the Berkeley University in California[25] found that "ever since humans developed agriculture, we've been transforming the planet and throwing the soil's nutrient cycle out of balance but because the changes happen slowly, often taking two to three generations to be noticed, people are not cognisant of the geological transformation taking place".

A 2004 study by the University of Texas[26] concludes that "efforts to breed new varieties of crops that provide greater yield, pest resistance and climate adaptability have allowed crops to grow bigger and more rapidly but their ability to manufacture or uptake nutrients has not kept pace with their rapid growth". A UK study found that between 1940 and 1990, nearly all vegetables studied had seen copper reduced by 76%, calcium by 46%, iron by 27%, magnesium by 24% and potassium by 16%. Heavy processing methods can remove nutrients from our food, too. Most health professionals will advise trying to obtain necessary nutrients

---

[25] Soil and human security in the 21st century - Ronald Amundson, Asmeret Asefaw Berhe, Jan W. Hopmans, Carolyn Olson, A. Ester Sztein, Donald L. Sparks - 'Science' May 2015
https://science.sciencemag.org/content/348/6235/1261071

[26] Changes in USDA food composition data for 43 garden crops, 1950 to 1999 - Donald R Davis, Melvin D Epp, Hugh D Riordan
https://pubmed.ncbi.nlm.nih.gov/15637215

from food before supplementing because foodstuffs are generally accompanied by many non-essential but beneficial nutrients such as hundreds of carotenoids, flavonoids, minerals and antioxidants that aren't in most supplements.

Supplements are a really efficient way of rectifying any deficiencies in the diet or where the body might need an extra boost. For example, hormonal imbalances might be quickly identified through taking the appropriate supplement and monitoring the response of symptoms. They are usually naturally produced and extracted and tend to be more gentle on the system than chemical alternatives. If a supplement is required, it is important to be specific about what is needed and advice from a kinesiologist, nutritionist or herbalist can be very useful. For example, there are three different types of magnesium supplement, not to mention combinations of the three! The right remedy for any individual condition should be carefully considered and the response closely monitored. Trial and error is often needed to get the type of supplement and the dosage right for optimal results. The presentation method of supplementation is also important. For example, vitamin D (great for all sorts of issues including autoimmune conditions) is best absorbed by the body as a spray into the inside of the mouth, whereas, a probiotic, which needs to make its way to the large intestine, will probably need a shell (capsule or similar) robust enough to withstand its passage through the intestinal tract.

The quality of supplements is greatly varied but not all are expensive. If in doubt, advice should be taken. This is because supplements do have an effect on the body, sometimes potently so, and we should therefore take care as with everything else, that what we consume will make us well and not unwell.

Hydration:

Finally, something to wash it all down with: water! Up to 60% of the human adult body is water.

According to H.H. Mitchell, Journal of Biological Chemistry[27] 158, the brain and heart are composed of 73% water and the lungs are about 83% water. The skin contains 64% water, muscles and kidneys are 79%, and even the bones are watery: 31%. The U.S. Geological Survey's (USGS) Water Science School refers to water as "a vital nutrient to the life of every cell, acting first as a building material for our bodies". It is estimated that the human body can last approximately three weeks without food but only three to four days without water.

Water is vital because:

- It regulates our internal body temperature by sweating and respiration.
- The carbohydrates and proteins that our bodies use as food are metabolised and transported by water in the bloodstream.
- It assists in flushing waste mainly through urination;
- Acts as a shock absorber for brain, spinal cord and foetus.

---

[27] https://www.usgs.gov/special-topic/water-science-school/science/water-you-water-and-human-body?qtscience_center_objects=0#qt-science_center_objects

- Forms saliva.
- Lubricates joints.

UK guidelines currently suggest a minimum intake of around 8 glasses of water each day (or around 1.5 - 2 litres), however, this will increase significantly if we undertake physical exercise or are in high temperatures due to fluid loss through sweat. Not getting enough water can be detrimental, potentially causing side effects like nausea, fatigue, constipation, headaches and dizziness. Good water intake levels are also linked to reduced swelling in the body and improved skin condition. Meeting our hydration needs really does support better health.

The path to good nutrition is long and can feel confusing. Just as our bodies are unique, so will the perfect nutritional input be. However, making changes to diet can have remarkable effects on physical and mental health as well as reducing and sometimes even eradicating existing health conditions. Starting with one small change can make a world of difference to our sense of wellbeing and as with all lifestyle changes, starting with something small and manageable will give a better prospect of maintaining the change and forming a habit. After two weeks, the habit will be formed and another change can be added in. Changes in diet should be seen as lifestyle changes. Try not to 'ban' anything as psychologically it immediately becomes more desirable. If we make decisions based on things we want to change and outcomes we want to experience, the changes and results fall in line with the brain's natural rewards system making us less likely to revert to old habits. And if old habits creep in again, don't punish or feel badly about it. Dietary habits are formed over a lifetime and they take time and persistence to change but it can be done, as everything can be, with commitment and persistence. Once the positive changes to wellbeing are in full flow, the only way is up...

MANTRA for good nutrition: I am the healthiest version of myself that I can be.

Exercise: On the left hand side of a page in a notebook, record your eating habits and food choices for a week. In the centre create a column to record exercise. On the right hand side, record sleep quality, stress levels and emotional state. At the end of the week, compare the columns and see if you can find any patterns or links between sleep, emotions, stress and the type of food that you eat.

Reflection: Next time you feel hungry, take yourself to a quiet place, close your eyes if you can and really connect with the feeling of hunger. Notice what it feels like in your body. Notice what it feels like in your mind. Is there a particular food that you are craving? What does that food contain? Is it sugar or is it something else, something that you could get from a more healthy or nutritious alternative source? Are you actually hungry or are you feeling something else like tiredness, sadness or boredom? Consider whether you are using food as a way to distract you from difficult feelings. If you are genuinely hungry, use this opportunity to think about what healthy food you can eat to satisfy that feeling. If you eat the healthier option and the feeling doesn't go away, reflect again. It's not hunger, it's something else: try to work out what. By building links between our body and mind and really connecting with how we feel, we can change our eating patterns considerably and improve our relationship with food.

Chapter 11
Mind

Mental health issues incorporate any issue related to our emotional, psychological and social well-being. Mental health affects how we think, feel and act. It also helps determine how we handle stress, relate to others and make choices. Mental health is important at every stage of life, from childhood and adolescence through adulthood. Unfortunately mental health issues are becoming increasingly prevalent. On average, it is estimated that at least one in four adults and one in ten children will experience a mental health issue in their lifetime. Mental health is multi faceted and it can be negatively impacted by a number of different factors. These include but are not limited to biological factors, such as genes or brain chemistry, and life experiences, such as trauma, abuse or excessive stress. Early warning signs that something is wrong include withdrawal from everyday patterns, disturbed sleep and energy levels, lack of emotion or feelings of hopelessness or self-harm, severe mood swings, increased conflict, use of alcohol or drugs as coping mechanisms or to escape reality, hearing voices or having irrational thoughts.

Physical environmental factors can contribute significantly to mental illness and this applies in particular to stress management. We can greatly increase our resilience to stressors in everyday life by maintaining good and healthy nutrition, a positive mindset, a healthy and hygienic sleep pattern and a physically and mentally active lifestyle. Social Environmental Factors can also be impactive upon mental health and resilience; socioeconomic status, race and ethnicity and support networks may also influence a person's ability to cope with stress. Social support and a sense of love or community is vital to maintaining strength and hope during hard times. Society and human conditioning can be extremely harmful to the less resilient amongst us when encountering stigma or a sense of being alone or 'not fitting in'. Other factors which increase the chances of mental health issues developing include family discord during childhood, the early loss of a parent, poverty and toxic relationships. Studies have shown that some of these socioeconomic factors can be counter balanced to some extend by developing spirituality or religious affiliation, having meaningful work or hobbies and a regime of proper and reliable self-care and / or relaxation. All of these factors must be taken into consideration when manging and treating mental illness.

It is a sad fact that the quality and availability of community mental health services in the UK continues to decline, especially for younger patients. Maintenance of good mental health is therefore more important than ever. An astonishing 70% of children and young people who experience a mental health problem have not had appropriate interventions at a sufficiently early age. The emotional wellbeing of both children and adults is just as important as physical health. Good mental health allows children and young people to develop the resilience to cope with whatever life throws at them and grow into well-rounded and healthy adults.

Things that can help keep children and young people mentally well are similar to adult factors but given their young developmental stage, they must also have the time and the freedom to play, indoors and outdoors, to take part in community activities, to be part of a supportive school environment and a family that gets along well most of the time and resolves problems in a healthy way. For children, who are still learning and trying to make sense of the world, their environment is critical to good long term mental health and resilience development. Children are accepting of the way things are. If they are exposed regularly to an unhealthy marriage, they will believe that this is what marriage should be. They have no blueprint to avoid it when they are older and so, even if by then they have realised that this is not something they want for themselves, they don't know what to look for to find something different. They are drawn as all humans are to what is familiar and therefore comfortable, even if the familiar is unhealthy or makes them feel sad. They end up in the very same relationship that they had been trying to avoid.

Children also need to develop positive feelings about themselves and others around them, especially anyone who they depend upon such as a parent or teacher. They must grow up feeling loved, trusted, understood, valued and safe in order to have good self-esteem and self-confidence. They have to feel that their life will be meaningful and purposeful to remain interested in themselves, hopeful and optimistic. In order to understand the importance of balance between work and fun, they must have opportunities to enjoy themselves and also to be able to learn and have opportunities to succeed and grow and to be rewarded for that. Having a sense of security and belonging and a sense of empowerment in their own lives will enable children to accept who they are and recognise that they have the strength to cope when something is wrong and the ability to solve problems. Although these childhood factors cannot prevent mental illness, providing this kind of healthy environment for children helps to insulate the mind against poor health right through to adulthood and beyond.

John Bowlby (1907–1990) was a psychoanalyst and believed that mental health and behavioural problems could be attributed to early childhood. He theorised that human beings are born with an innate psychobiological system (the attachment behavioural system) that motivates them to seek closeness with significant others (attachment figures such as parents) in times of need. He also outlined major individual differences in the functioning of individuals who develop a healthy and an unhealthy attachment system. He found that children who had healthy attachment (i.e. parents who are available in times of need and who are sensitive and responsive to requests for closeness and support) tend to develop a stable sense of attachment, security and build positive mental feelings in the child about himself and others. In contrast, when a child's attachment figures are not reliably available and supportive, attempts to be close to them fail to relieve distress, the security they may have felt is undermined and an unhealthy and negative view is created in the child, both of himself and others. Bowlby considered that unhealthy attachment in childhood greatly increased the likelihood of later emotional problems, an inability to adjust to change and lower resilience to mental health issues.

A 2012 study by the World Psychiatric Association[28] identified that attachment-related issues in individuals change how we are able to cope with stress, manage distress and retain psychological resilience. The study concluded that attachment insecurities – called attachment anxiety and avoidance within the theory – are associated with mental health disorders and that increases in attachment security are an important part of successfully treating these disorders.

The behaviour patterns that result from childhood insecurity or trauma can be varied but are rarely healthy. They may include addictive type behaviours with drugs or alcohol or shopping or gambling which are designed to create dopamine 'highs' or to avoid feeling strong emotions. We may recognise patterns of unhealthy behaviours in our own relationships. We may experience a sense of distance, which we don't know how to fix, or perhaps feel a sense of discomfort in how we react to others. We may have obsessive, compulsive type behaviours which bind us to patterns we would rather not follow any more. Whatever issue may have been created for us (and in the case of childhood trauma or insecurity those issues are absolutely NOT of our creation!), it can be fixed with commitment and the right help. Resolution does mean that we have to speak out, however, to ask for help and to seek support for ourselves. This takes great courage and strength. Unpicking mental health issues can be difficult but the efforts are well worth the reward to take control back over our thought processes and mood and to

---

[28] World Psychiatry. 2012 Feb; doi: 10. 1016/j.wpsyc.2012.01.003 - An attachment perspective on psychopathology : Mario Mikulincer and Philip R. Shaver

choose the behaviours we want to keep in our lives and those that we want to discard.

Many of us are so busy racing through life at an unsustainable pace that we have never stopped to actually get to know ourselves or to reflect upon why we do the things we do, why we think the way we think and whether we want to continue in those patterns of behaviour. Spending time alone, walking, meditating or just doing something enjoyable is a great opportunity to test whether you actually like spending time with yourself. If not, why not? What is it about yourself that you would wish to change?

Self-reflection is the only way to develop and spiritually grow as an adult and can only be achieved over time, and with commitment, focus and honesty. If we are not aware of our unhealthy behaviour, we cannot identify this as an area that needs work. If we develop the ability to explore ourselves with honesty and compassion and with unclouded vision, we can identify the changes we need to make to take good care of ourselves. It can be extremely difficult to identify things that we don't like about ourselves and to have the courage to acknowledge that we are not as strong or as resilient as we may like to believe. We have to accept fragility. Recognising webs or patterns of behaviour which are not healthy for us is the first step. If we can go on to develop insight, to work out where they came from and whether they are built on principles which are true or by which we want to continue to live by, we can develop an understanding of whether the way that we are living will ever actually bring happiness. As we become more conscious about how we are living we develop an ability to reframe the relationships, patterns and environment around us to facilitate our new chosen life.

Some of this work to change behavioural patterns and develop resilience will require us to get comfortable with being uncomfortable! In order to really understand the negativity that we live with, we have to explore it. This can make us feel uneasy and for much of the time it forces us to engage rather than use avoidance strategies. We cannot use our usual distraction techniques of alcohol or shopping or sex and instead have to sit with how it feels to face our feelings instead. What we create during this process is an understanding that we are strong enough to manage the negative feeling and also, in sitting with it, we learn that it will pass without catastrophe. As we develop and grow we may no longer fit with friendship groups built around old patterns. We may need to alter the way that we interact with family as we create a healthy environment and establish and maintain boundaries. This process can also be difficult and support from our usual sources may not be forthcoming. Trust that there will be new conncctions and support to fill the space that the old ones left behind. However challenging the process may appear, it is always worth the investment to create a life of our choosing and the possibility of contentment, peace and happiness.

The process of addressing trauma and diagnosed psychological and psychiatric conditions is, of course, much more case specific and should be undertaken with professional support. The importance of actually addressing any mental health issue remains the same whatever the diagnosis. It is critical to our mental health but also to our overall physical health that we face it. Don't let it get stuck inside! If negative responses are not expressed, they will stagnate in the body, mind and cause illness. Finding a way to process or reframe old experiences and trauma will help develop strategies for managing any future issue that arises and so; once the backlog has cleared, we will be free to manage the good and the bad experiences of life in a more conscious and mindful way. We get rid of the misconceptions that we developed in childhood because of our confused and immature thinking and learn to establish the difference between what feels real to us and is real and what feels real to us but is untrue (the product of our unhealthy thinking or coping mechanisms).

In life there will always be pain but if we allow it to pass through us, the discomfort leaves us and we are free of it forever. If we resist pain, it makes us suffer as it stagnates and grows and causes on-going worry and upset. Pain plus resistance equals suffering. Pain plus acceptance equals freedom. Stagnated trauma breeds sickness for body and mind and should most definitely be avoided!

Our minds are truly powerful machines and have an astonishing impact upon our general sense of wellbeing. The power of thought is a remarkable tool in the wellbeing toolkit. As the philosophical writer James Allen said on 1903 in his book *As a Man Thinketh*[29], the truth for every man and woman is that

"they themselves are makers of themselves, by virtue of the thoughts which they choose and encourage".

He believed that the mind is the 'master weaver' of character and circumstance and that the power of thoughts and

---

[29] 'As a man thinketh', James Allen

deeds had the ability to bring ignorance and pain or enlightenment and happiness. The title, which comes from the Bible verse,

"As a man thinketh in his heart so he is"

epitomises the theme of the book. The character of a person is said to be the sum total of all his thoughts. Allen takes the theory a step further, explaining how positive thinking causes us to take positive action in our circumstances and how strong and happy thoughts build a strong body in 'vigour and grace'.

Modern physiological thinking supports this theory. Barbara Frederickson, psychologist, published a landmark paper revisited in 2001[30]. She concluded that "because positive emotions arise in response to broad opportunities rather than narrowly focused threats, positive emotions momentarily broaden people's attention and thinking, enabling them to draw on higher-level connections and a wider-than-usual range of thoughts or ideas. In turn, these broadened outlooks often help people to discover and build consequential personal resources and skills. These resources can be cognitive, like the ability to mindfully attend to the present moment; psychological, like the ability to maintain a sense of mastery over environmental challenges; social, like

---

[30] Fredrickson, B. L., Cohn, M. A., Coffey, K. A., Pek, J., & Finkel, S. M. (2008). Open hearts build lives: Positive emotions, induced through loving-kindness meditation, build consequential personal resources. Journal of Personality and Social Psychology, 95(5), 1045–1062. https://doi.org/10.1037/a0013262

the ability to give and receive emotional support or physical, like the ability to ward off the common cold. People with these resources are more likely to effectively meet life's challenges and take advantage of its opportunities, becoming successful, healthy and happy in the months and years to come. The personal resources accrued, often unintentionally through frequent experiences of positive emotions are key to developing and building upon increases in well-being. Put simply, the broaden-and-build theory states that positive emotions widen people's outlooks in ways that little by little, reshape who they are."

Scientifically proven ways of creating positive emotions in ourselves include:

- **Meditation:** People who meditate daily are proven to display more positive emotions than those who do not and benefit from life skills such as mindfulness, purpose in life, social support and decreased rates of illness.
- **Writing a gratitude journal or positive thoughts journal:** A study in the *Journal of Research in Personality* found that writing about positive experiences daily led to improved mood levels, fewer medical appointments and fewer illnesses.
- **Making time for fun:** Hobbies and leisure activities led to more enjoyment which lifts mood and increases physical resilience as well as allowing us to develop new skills.

Studies have also shown that our environment has a measurable impact on our psychology. Both American studies, one showed that subjects holding a warm drink[31] when having a conversation were significantly more likely to offer warm and friendly conversation than those who did not hold the drink. A second proved that a group of students had more creative ideas and had improved brain function when they sat OUTSIDE a man-made 'box' than they were when they sitting INSIDE it, perceiving themselves to be closed in and restricted[32]. Small changes in our environment really can affect our thought processes and brain function. Next time creativity is called for, step outside the office and witness the creativity that the perception of freedom brings! This may explain why runners describe 'clearing their heads' when out pounding the pavement. It also underlines the importance of developing the skill of 'screening out the noise', or putting any unnecessary thoughts out of our heads when they begin to disrupt us.

It is extremely common for us humans to out-source our wellbeing to external factors. We may feel that we will be happy if... we get that new job, we find love, we earn more money. We often attach our ability to 'be ok' to something external happening. If we have no control over that external

---

[31] Experiencing physical warmth promotes interpersonal warmth : Lawrence E. Williams and John A. Bargh - Department of Psychology, Yale University.
https://science.sciencemag.org/content/sci/suppl/2008/10/23/322.5901.606.DC1/Williams.SOM.pdf

[32] Creativity in the Wild: Improving Creative Reasoning through Immersion in Natural Settings - Ruth Ann Atchley, David L. Strayer, and Paul Atchley
https://www.ncbi.nlm.nih.gov/pmc/articles/PMC3520840/

factor, whether or not it actually ever happens, we give away control over our sense of wellness. It is a crucial realisation everyone already has everything we need inside of us. We are born with innate systems that are specifically designed to ensure our wellbeing and health is maintained. We lose connection with our ability to manage our own sense of wellness through conditioning and a loss of empowerment. Our sense of feeling out of control becomes our reality but we can reverse this process, too if we so choose. Change is possible with a shift in mindset to one of positivity and choice and by using that sense of empowerment to recognise what is not beneficial and to step away from old and limiting patterns of thought or behaviour.

Controlling our thoughts is a very important skill in management of good mental health. Noticing when our minds have taken us back to an unhappy memory or to a future worry keeps our thinking in the moment and focussed on the topic of our choice. It is hugely empowering and builds self-esteem and confidence. It is a well proven way to stay positive in mind set and to be happier as a result. Mindfulness is an excellent way of mastering thought patterns as is meditation and yoga.

Sat Bir Singh Khalsa, PhD, Assistant Professor of Medicine and Neurologist at Harvard Medical School describes the four essential components that make yoga what it is: The first is the physical postures which promote movement, controlled breathing and exercise techniques working the body to improve global functioning. The second is building the ability to control and self-regulate emotional and internal stress responses, increasing resilience to stress in the face of emotions. Thirdly, Yoga cultivates mind-body awareness by helping us to feel what's going on in our bodies and to observe the flow of thoughts in our minds without becoming attached to them. Cultivation of mind-body awareness can increase mindfulness that in turn can change behaviours in a positive way. Finally, Yoga also encourages the experience of deeper spiritual states. This kind of experience can be transformative with people to help drive them towards more positive purpose.

Professor Khalsa's research in field of yoga in depression and anxiety disorders showed a reduction of symptoms of 33% in group of yoga practitioners compared to ordinary medicinal approaches. The yoga group also showed increases in resilience, reported increased positive experiences and a decrease in negative experiences. After just 12 minutes per day for 6 weeks, the yoga practitioners also showed improvements in mental health generally. Evidence supports the suggestion that doing something including movement, breathing techniques, mindful attention and relaxation can make extraordinary differences to mental health.

Remarkably, science is now able to demonstrate that not only does yoga (or meditation practice) enable people to manage stress and emotion, it can actually change brain activity and over time can change brain structure. Changes in the stress management system and nervous system can actually be measured. Professor Khalsa describes the scientific principle as the creation of space. He explains that by creating space in mind and body, old blockages can be flushed out of the system. Mediation is about emptying the mind. Vassanas (yoga positions) create much needed space in the body, allowing energy to flow. For those who think that this is fanciful, the Professor explains that on a physical level, this is simply the body establishing new connections. Blood vessels and nerves, all carry energy through the body such as molecules like ATP or glucose (Adenosine triphosphate, an energy carrying molecule found in the cells of all living things. ATP captures chemical energy obtained from the breakdown of food molecules and releases it to fuel other cellular processes). The Professor clarifies that Prana is simply electro-magnetic heat flowing through the body in molecules like ATP or glucose and that when we have that energy freely flowing through the body we are much more likely to have good health.

Neurologically speaking, he explains that yoga forces us to constantly create physical challenge. As the pre frontal cortex of our brain is working to redirect attention to that physical stress response, we are also working on our emotional stress response by calming ourselves down. Through breathing techniques, we bring out the parasympathetic nervous system signal despite the stress that our bodies are experiencing. Regular practice creates habit and these healthy habits can be applied in everyday life. When faced with a stressful situation outside of the yoga or meditation studio, we can still respond with slow breath and redirected attention, keep calm and not react impulsively.

The emerging science of Epigenetics explores how individuals may be able to change the expression of our DNA or how our DNA affects us without changing the actual DNA code itself. An example of this is having an increased likelihood of developing heart disease in our DNA but avoiding the 'expression' of this or stopping actually happening through healthy living, diet and exercise. Epigenetics in psychology explains how the expression of genes is influenced by experiences and the environment to produce individual differences in behaviour, cognition, personality and mental health. The more power we have in our consciousness mind, therefore, the more power we have in our life. According to epigenetics, mood is the ultimate control of health as such a significant percentage of illnesses are thought to be related to stress.

So, put simply and eloquently by Professor Khalsa,[33]

"Yoga and meditation have the capacity to change brain structure, morality, nervous system and physiology by creating new transmitters and molecules in the brain as well as enhancing the immune response and reduce things like inflammation. Yoga is no longer just a hobby. Science is discovering that it can create real biological change at the cellular and molecular level as well as behavioural change and significant improvements in mental health."

Practices like yoga and meditation also help improve self-control, inside and outside of the studio. In their ground breaking work, scientists at the McGill University have clearly identified the parts of the brain involved in decisions

---

[33] Sat Bir Singh Khalsa is a researcher in the field of body mind medicine, specialising in yoga therapy, Assistant Professor of Medicine at Harvard Medical School and an Associate Neuroscientist (since 1998) in the Division of Sleep and Circadian Disorders, at the Departments of Medicine and Neurology, Boston

that call for delayed gratification[34]. They discovered that the hippocampus (associated with memory) and the nucleus accumbens (associated with pleasure) work together in making critical decisions related to gratification, delayed or otherwise. The connection between the two enables rationalisation of thought and helps us to prioritise long term goals over short term gratification. This is especially useful when we are trying to resist that piece of cake in favour of our health or figure or whether to choose immediate praise for rapidly completing a work project over the longer term damage to our health that the associated stress would bring to our lives. These studies also have potential benefit in understanding and treating a range of neuropsychiatric disorders including ADHD, eating and anxiety disorders and indeed maladaptive daily decision making about drug or alcohol use, gambling, food or credit card binges.

By strengthening the relationship between the hippocampus and nucleus accumbens, simply by using willpower to create habitual behaviour, we can improve our prospects of choosing our longer term goals over immediate gratification even when we are tired, distracted or less resilient to temptation.

Our mind is an extremely powerful machine. When used in a conscious way and especially when in sync with our extraordinary bodies, it can create remarkable changes. These are amplified and accelerated when we place ourselves in an environment which supports the changes that we are making.

---

[34] Waiting for pleasure : Brain structures involved in delayed gratification identified; implications for range of psychiatric disorders - August 2015 - McGill University

Never underestimate the power of thought. It can be used to forcefully drive positive change but can also draw us into a cycle of negativity and pessimism if left unchecked. It is for that reason that we must be as conscious and mindful in our thinking as possible.

As Lao Tzu, Chinese philosopher credited with founding the philosophical system of Taoism, so profoundly said,

"Watch your thoughts, they become your words; watch your words, they become your actions; watch your actions, they become your habits; watch your habits, they become your character; watch your character, it becomes your destiny."

MANTRA for positive mental health: I change my thoughts; I change my world.

Exercise: Score yourself 1–5 in the following areas, 1 being not at all and 5 being always:

1. When I set myself a goal, I usually achieve it.
2. I feel that my life has meaning and purpose.
3. I look at life's challenges as opportunities for growth and learning.
4. When things get tough, I have friends and family that I can talk to.
5. When I feel overwhelmed, I understand the reasons for feeling that way.
6. I fall back on my faith in something outside of myself.
7. I am controlled and conscious in my response to stress or in a crisis.

8. I take care of myself by eating well, sleeping enough and exercising regularly.
9. I can see the funny side of challenging situations.
10. I can adapt to change and uncertainty.

A total score over 40 indicates resilience and shows evidence of good coping strategies. Any question that scored four or less is an area where there is room for improvement.

Reflection: Take one area from the exercise above for which you scored yourself four or less and reflect upon what changes you could make in your life to increase that score. Think about whether others would score you higher than you have scored yourself (which indicates that it may be a mindset change that is needed or greater self-esteem). You may discover that the action required to increase a score in one area actually increased your score in multiple areas. Make the changes that you have identified and test yourself again in a month's time. How different is your score? Can you feel a difference in your sense of wellbeing and happiness as a result of the changes that you have made?

Chapter 12
Body

In times gone by, we used our bodies very differently than we do today. Much of the work available was manual labour. There were no such things as computers or mobile phones and so we spent much more time outdoors, socialising, perhaps playing sport or leisure activities such as playing cards, knitting and so on. These days, we spend much more time 'in our heads', working on computer screens and in desk jobs, requiring us to sit still for hours and hours at a time. When we play sport or enjoy leisure activities, it is often to 'clear' our busy mind or to 'forget about' or 'unwind from' the day. As a result of this paradigm shift in the way we live, our minds have become disconnected from our physical bodies in so many ways. We no longer think of ourselves as 'being' our bodies or our souls but rather as 'being' what is in our minds. The disconnect that results tends to make us observe our bodies objectively, liking or disliking our physical form on the basis of what we think others see rather than recognising the service that our bodies provide for us.

This disconnect is evidence from our experiences of modern life. So much of our experience is visual and aural and through a screen. Our experience of smell and touch, or how something makes us feel is much more limited. We have learned to become less attuned to those more meaningful elements of life which give us a more rounded and sensory experience of the world. When we consider that the sense of smell is the one which is most likely to provoke an emotional response within us and to invoke memories, it becomes clear that our experience of a two-dimensional world is much less satisfying or meaningful than the full 4D version that we could have. It is important for our own sense of wellbeing and happiness to experience our lives through our bodies and all of our senses as well as through our minds as much as we possibly can.

Our bodies are truly miraculous machines that are at our disposal every moment of the day. Our body does its very best to be what it thinks we want it to be. If we overeat, it gains weight. If we are active, it grows fitter. If we nourish it, it is refreshed. If we abuse it, it cannot function well. If we neglect it over time, it will fail eventually. It is important to understand that the output from our bodies will, generally speaking, directly reflect what we put in. Our body is our own individual responsibility and in taking the very best possible care of it, we stand the best chance of getting the best possible results from it, for life.

The importance of physical health on general wellbeing is generally well accepted. The physical body needs to be maintained if it is to function at an optimum state. Maintenance includes much more than just physical exercise, however. Of course, exercise is essential for cardio health and retention of muscle mass. Through physical exertion we can build strength and stamina, conditioning and toning our bodies to make them appear slimmer or more muscular, to take a chosen form. Exercise can also provide an outlet for relieving stress and quieting the mind. However, true and enduring maintenance of our physical bodies also includes good nutrition and plentiful sleep. Without these two elements, the body cannot reach optimal performance level, let alone maintain it.

It is essential to be aware of the inextricable links between mind and body if we are to remain healthy. Poor physical self-care is linked with poor self-esteem, which in turn is linked to poor outcomes in mental health maintenance. A 2018 study found that genetic variants linked to high BMI can lead to mental health issues. We know that depression is more common among people who are obese. But previous studies had not been able to determine whether there is a direct cause and effect relationship. So it could be the case that depression causes weight gain rather than the other way around or indeed both could be true. It is also possible that complications associated with obesity such as type 2 diabetes are contributing to depression rather than the obesity itself. However, the study did provide results that suggest that obesity influences depression risk through psychological rather than metabolic changes; at least in some cases.[35]

People who exercise regularly have a lower risk of developing many long-term (chronic) conditions such as heart disease, type 2 diabetes, stroke and some cancers. Research

---

[35] Using genetics to understand the causal influence of higher BMI on depression - Jessica Tyrrell, Anwar Mulugeta, Andrew R Wood, Ang Zhou,et al. nternational Journal of Epidemiology, Volume 48, Issue 3, June 2019, Pages 834–848, https://doi.org/10.1093/ije/dyy223

shows that physical activity can also boost self-esteem, mood, sleep quality and energy as well as reducing your risk of stress, depression, dementia and Alzheimer's disease. The NHS confirm that people who do regular physical activity have:

- Up to a 35% lower risk of coronary heart disease and stroke
- Up to a 50% lower risk of type 2 diabetes
- Up to a 50% lower risk of colon cancer
- Up to a 20% lower risk of breast cancer
- A 30% lower risk of early death
- Up to an 83% lower risk of osteoarthritis
- Up to a 68% lower risk of hip fracture
- A 30% lower risk of falls in older adults
- Up to a 30% lower risk of depression
- Up to a 30% lower risk of dementia

The NHS website notes that "exercise is the miracle cure we've always had but for too long, we've neglected to take our recommended dose. Our health is now suffering as a consequence." It recommends 150 minutes of moderate or vigorous intensity exercise per week, spread over a variety of activities. Moderate exercise is where we can still speak but wouldn't be able to sing the lyrics to a song. High intensity exercise prevents us from speaking during our workout. If our health is otherwise good, generally speaking, the higher the intensity exercise, the greater the health benefits. It is important to make sure that we are not sedentary for the remainder of the week, even if we are meeting our recommended 150 minutes of exercise. Remaining regularly active is the key to better physical health.

Being aware of external stressors, nutritional deficiencies and environmental toxins is the first step to reducing the impact that they have on our bodies. Making small changes the way that we live has a huge impact over the course of our lifetime. For example, changing to a non-aluminium deodorant will prevent application of a toxic metal to our skin which can be absorbed into our bodies. Of course, the daily amount that we apply cannot possibly be harmful. However, over the course of 70 years, we will apply this tiny amount over 25,000 times! The accumulating impact of that may well be harmful. The same can be said for carefully washing fruit and veg to remove pesticides before eating or not drinking from plastic water bottles. It is the repeated small doses of harmful substances that can cause poor health outcomes in the longer term.

Biohacking is the practice of making small, incremental dietary or lifestyle changes to change the body's responses and to make small but consistent improvements in health and well-being. This can be anything from supplementing, red-light therapy and hormone manipulation to alternative and innovative therapies. The practice is becoming increasingly popular as we become more aware of the impact of our current lifestyles on our health and realise that we can reverse it by taking control of what we consume and what we expose ourselves to environmentally and socially.

Another revolutionary means of taking control over the way our bodies behave is Epigenetics. Epigenetics is closely related to Genetics. We know that genetics is the study of our DNA which is the 'life code' that makes us who we are and which contains instructions to tell our cells how to behave. Epigenetics is the study of systems within our body (biological mechanisms) that will switch genes on and off and so determine whether our cells will do what they are told to do by our genes. There are a number of things that can affect whether our cells do what our genes tell them to do. What we eat, where and how we live, the people and environment we create for ourselves, how we sleep and exercise can all cause chemical modifications around the genes over time. Those chemical modifications can change the way that cells behave, so effectively turning genes on or off in the longer term. In certain diseases such as genetically predisposed cancer or Alzheimer's, some genes are already switched into the opposite state, predisposed away from 'healthy' and towards disease development. If we could map or harness the relevant epigenetic code, we could theoretically switch the gene the other way through changes in our environment over time. The theory of epigenetics offers endless possibilities. It is encased in common sense. It is another exaple of the old adage: We are the product of our environment. If we control that environment, we become much more empowered in controlling what we become. This has a ripple effect on our mental health too.

The environment we create around us shapes the chemical balance in our bodies. From endorphin boosting gratitude journals (which improves happiness and psycopathology, personality, relationships, health, well-being and functioning) to the sense of community we foster with our friends (creating a sense of strength and resilience which translates to improved actual physical strength), it all either gives back to us piece by piece or takes away. Immersing ourselves in an environment filled with positivity cannot help but make our sense of happiness and wellbeing soar. Getting outside is one quick and easy way to help body and mind feel better, increase productivity and creativity and reduce stress.

Forest bathing is gaining popularity the world over, especially in Eastern regions where traditional medicine has been practiced for centuries and the natural healing power of the body is arguably better understood. In Japan, 'shinrin-yoku' or 'forest-bathing' is considered a form of preventative medicine. Walking in nature has been found to have a memory boosting, de-stressing effect, can reduce inflammation in the body (prolonged inflammation is associated with autoimmune disorders, inflammatory bowel disease, depression and cancer), can eliminate fatigue and fight depression and anxiety. In office workers, even a window view of nature or looking at a picture of nature has been associated in studies with lower stress and higher job satisfaction. One Japanese study found that along with decreasing stress hormone concentrations by more than 15%, a walk in the forest lowered participants' average pulse by almost 4% and blood pressure by just over 2%.[36]

Remarkably, whilst research is still in its earliest phases, evidence is emerging that spending time in nature – in forests, in particular – may stimulate the production of anti-cancer proteins. Studies in Japan have also discovered that areas with

---

[36] The physiological effects of Shinrin-yoku (taking in the forest atmosphere or forest bathing): evidence from field experiments in 24 forests across Japan - Bum Jin Park, Yuko Tsunetsugu, Tamami Kasetani,Takahide Kagawa,and Yoshifumi Miyazaki
https://www.ncbi.nlm.nih.gov/pmc/articles/PMC2793346/

greater forest coverage have reduced mortality from a wide variety of cancers[37]. This change in cellular activity caused by our environment is one that we can each choose as often as time will permit. An Environmental Health Perspectives study found a connection between exposure to 'greenness' and a 12% lower mortality rate. The biggest improvements were related to reduced risk of death from cancer, lung disease and kidney disease.[38]

The reasons for this connection are currently unclear. Speculative theories include:

1. Improved body / mind connection

Being outdoors helps us to slow down, connect our minds, bodies and souls together again, creates the feeling of space and promotes relaxation. The composite parts of our body can sync together again, working in harmony rather than against each other as so often happens during a busy stressful life.

---

[37] Forest bathing enhances human natural killer activity and expression of anti-cancer proteins - Q Li, K Morimoto, A Nakadai, H Inagaki, M Katsumata et al -opathol Pharmacol Apr-Jun 2007 https://pubmed.ncbi.nlm.nih.gov/17903349/

[38] Exposure to Greenness and Mortality in a Nationwide Prospective Cohort Study of Women - Peter James, Jaime E. Hart, Rachel F. Banay, Francine Laden September 2016
https://ehp.niehs.nih.gov/doi/10.1289/ehp.1510363

2. Plant secretions

Research in 2018 showed that after 'forest bathing', our bodies carry increased numbers of natural killer (NK) cells, which remain notably elevated for seven days afterwards. NK cells are an essential lymphocyte that boosts the immune system defences against viruses and cancers. This is thought by researchers to be the result of exposure to phytoncides, a natural substance, which is emitted by the forest trees and plants. The same effect can be created to a lesser extent by filling our homes with plants, increasing our daily exposure to phytoncides and indeed maintaining our connection to nature with all of the health and wellbeing benefits that brings. (Nurturing plants has also been found to have a positive effect on psychological wellbeing).

3. Vibrations

All things in the universe are constantly in vibrating at different frequencies, even when we cannot see it with the naked eye. This includes human beings, man-made matter and everything in nature. When differently vibrating entities come closer to one another, their vibrations very often begin to sync, sometimes in ways that can seem mysterious. This is known as 'the phenomenon of spontaneous self-organisation'. When outside in nature, our body begins to sync with the Earth's frequency (approximately 7.83 hertz) and at that frequency, the body is generally able to restore and heal itself more effectively. This vibrational frequency is the natural frequency of the brain's alpha wave, a state which we rest in when relaxed but not quite in a meditative state.

4. Soil connection

A bacterium in soil, Mycobacterium vaccae, has been found to trigger the release of seratonin, the chemical in our bodies which improves mood and possibly brain function too. Any contact with soil, whether through picnicking, play or gardening is beneficial. Any asthma sufferers take note: Recent research has also found that exposure to bacteria in soil may reduce the risk of asthma!

The mind-body connection is of crucial importance in processing trauma. Despite popular belief, feelings are not experienced in the mind but in the body. Our body physically reacts to our life experiences, especially traumatic or psychologically impactive ones. This process is linked to the 'fight or flight' response in the nervous system and creates energy in the body which has to be processed properly if it is not to become 'stuck'. Unresolved and unprocessed trauma is not only harmful for the psychological system and mental health but is crucial for long term physical health too. Healthy coping mechanisms, boundaries and general self-care are essential if we are to avoid chronic physical disease.

So physical wellness involves a great deal more than hitting the gym three times per week and eating the right food! Physical exercise creates its own natural tension in the muscles. We all understand and accept the importance of stretching and make space after a workout to create balance in the physical body and improve our natural and energetic flow. It is also important to make space from the tension that our busy lives create. Through practices such as yoga, pilates, meditation or spending time in nature, we can create the balance required to improve our natural rhythm, to release blockages and prevent stagnation and sickness.

There is so much that we can do to help our dutiful bodies to help us. We have a choice to live better in so many ways. Any change is a positive move towards improved health and wellbeing and, in turn, greater balance, happiness and fulfilment.

MANTRA for physical health: I am safe. I am happy. I am healthy.

Exercise: Take a walk in nature with a difference! Take yourself to a forest or woodland if possible but into a park or green area if not. Instead of simply looking at what is around you, actually experience it with all of your senses. Explore how the different plants and flowers feel and smell, notice the texture of their leaves and the differences in their colours. Now find somewhere to take a seat. Look at where you are sitting. If it is grass, look at the different plants that appear within in. If it is a tree stump or log, feel how it is to sit on top of it. Is it covered in moss or leaves or bark? Is it damp or dry? What surrounds the place where you sit? What can you see? How much light or sunshine would there be during the day? Would there be a clear view of the moon and stars at night time? Now choose a tree or plant, something that stands out to you. Go and sit beside it. Think about how this plant or tree is rooted in the ground and cannot move from its spot. Think about the advantages to being in this place forever and the advantages of being rooted. Now think about the advantages of being able to move freely. Think about the differences in plant life and what it needs to flourish compared with what you need. Think about how your life is linked to the life of the plants around you as part of the food chain and as part of a co-dependent universe. Think about how you uniquely fit into the universe and all of its vastness. Think about the place of your chosen plant or tree; still completely unique. Close your eyes for five minutes or longer if you choose. Feel the sun or breeze or rain on your face. Breath in the clean air and be thankful for all that you are. You are uniquely and perfectly you.

Reflection: Think back to a time in your life when you have been the healthiest or fittest that you have ever been. What was going on for you at that time? What were your responsibilities? What was your job? How did you manage to prioritise your health in the way that you did? How was your general sense of flow? Are there things that you could do now to prioritise your health a little higher? What stops you from accessing better health and fitness. Is there something else that you spend time doing that you could replace with exercise?

Chapter 13
Soul

Whatever our religious beliefs, we all have a sense of being an individual and acknowledge our absolute uniqueness. We experience unique connections with others. We have thoughts, feelings and desires which shape us. We have a sense of knowing sometimes before things happen. We have likes and dislikes which differ from our caregivers who raised us and which cannot be explained by our DNA. These elements are driven by the energy that shapes our personality from the moment that we are born. Whether we believe in the power of the universe, a pre-written destiny or in deities or whether we think that we are individually creating and shaping our existence ourselves, it does not matter. We all have an energy within us and around us that we cannot explain. This is often referred to as our 'spirit' 'life-force' or 'soul'.

When our soul is unsettled, our thoughts, feelings and desires are disturbed. We may feel distressed or sense discomfort but not be able to understand why. We may feel unable to move forward but cannot identify what is preventing us from doing so. We may be very easily distracted, uncomfortable, fixated, afraid, worried or conflicted. We may neglect ourselves, fall out of good self-care habits or procrastinate. Our friendships and relationships may begin to suffer. When our soul is not settled and in sync with our body and mind, the sense of imbalance can feel overwhelming and, at times, crippling.

In the Buddhist faith, there are six realms. One is described as the Realm of the Hungry Ghosts. The ghosts represent the human condition of always craving something more and never feeling satisfied. Sometimes referred to as the 'hole in the soul' in psychological circles, this creates a sense of constant searching, moving through life as though something is missing and trying to fill the hole with something, anything to make the feeling go away. We harbour a real feeling of failure or disappointment that our lives aren't turning out the way we wanted. All human beings experience this to some degree. Feeling that 'I need something more to be OK', encourages us to indulge in our vices which in turn, ironically, prevent us from living a full and authentic life. When we do capitulate and give in to our vices to sooth ourselves, we judge ourselves for doing so. This makes the feeling of failure or not being good enough even worse! And so the cycle continues…

In a world where we are constantly encouraged by social media to compare ourselves to the perceived successes of others, it can be very difficult not to try to feed those ghosts sometimes! Through the screens that surround us in so many aspects of our life, the world invades. Messages are bombarding us from every angle to like this or to buy that. To strive to be this way or to want to be that way. There is no discernible boundary between fact and fiction. We cannot easily identify what is reliable, dependable and true. It is now so difficult for our brains to make sense of the world and an even greater challenge to find our place amongst it all.

In 2019, the 7th UN World Happiness Report was published and made clear links between the prevalence of digital media, instance of addiction and an absence of happiness. It is no coincidence that these elements are linked. They combine to fuel the hungry ghosts and leave us chasing something that we can never attain.

In these moments of dissatisfaction with life, it can be tempting to distract ourselves further or to turn back to old ways of self-soothing or self-medicating such as alcohol, drugs, shopping or other addictive behaviours. The immediate draw is outwards because whether we are able to acknowledge it or not, our soul can feel that the anguish is coming from within. If we are able to find the courage to look inwards, however, to sit with the discomfort then we begin to actually see what is causing the problem. By quieting the mind and screening out the noise, the fog clears, we find clarity. With clarity generally comes a wisdom to understand how to resolve the discontent or to know where else we might look for answers.

So many people around the world have found a way to reconnect with their soul and so to quiet the ghosts and find contentment. They all have one thing in common; they have found a way to be thankful for what they have and to be satisfied with enough.

In her truly beautiful book 'Wabi Sabi' Beth Kempton tries to explain this ancient Japanese concept to a Western audience. She writes,

"Wabi Sabi is a state of the heart…it is an intuitive response that reflects the true nature of life…an acceptance and appreciation of the impermanent and imperfect and incomplete nature of everything…it is the recognition of the gifts of simple, slow and natural living…The secret of Wabi Sabi lies in seeing the world not with the logical mind but with the feeling of the heart."[39]

The feeling of Wabi Sabi, a moment of contentment in an imperfect world requires connection between mind, body and soul. It requires us to look inward to recognise beauty in what is already present without wishing it was different or that it was something else instead. There is no FOMO (fear of missing out) in Wabi Sabi. In Wabi Sabi, everything we ever need is already in side of each of us. It is already present in our soul.

It is often necessary for us to experience a crisis to recognise the need to adjust our priorities. The shock of a bereavement or an illness in the family can awaken us to what is really important to us; to see the value of experience, connection and the real and priceless cost of wasting time on things that do not matter. A useful exercise to feel this surge of realisation is to stand facing someone who is important to you. Say to one another 'I am going to die' Then say to one another, 'and you are going to die'. Embrace the person meaningfully as you say, 'these precious moments'. It is an exercise in recognising what enriches our soul rather than what feeds our ego.

---

[39] Wabi Sabi" by Beth Kempton

Our egos are powerful drivers and often work in direct conflict with our soul. If we want to keep our soul in balance, it is important to check in with ourselves regularly during quieter moments to make sure that the path we are following is still authentic and the right one for us. We must never be afraid to change direction in anything and trust and believe in ourselves and in our intuition. If we are patient with ourselves, we will learn the lessons meant for us. Only then will they stop repeating. If we can stop trying to control everything and to force things into being that are not meant to be, our spirit has space to recognise what we need. This more relaxed and ultimately more fulfilling and satisfying approach to life goes hand in hand with being grateful for what we already have, as we finally stop chasing what may not be meant for us.

Studies have identified nine 'Blue Zone' communities of the world who have a much higher life expectancy that average. The Blue Zone regions are home to some of the oldest and healthiest people in the world. Their lifestyles differ in some ways but the common themes that unite their lifestyles are a mostly plant-based diet, daily exercise or movement, moderate alcohol consumption, prioritising sleep and enduring and positive spiritual, family and social networks. In all of these remarkable cultures, the elderly members are revered for their wisdom and continue to be purposeful and happy with a genuine sense of belonging and satisfaction.

If we are to live long then we must live well. In a modern world, it is easy to think that there must be a tension between living life to the full and longevity but this is not the case. A healthy and satisfied life does not involve risk taking behaviour or emotional drama. If we trust our intuition to guide us, trust in our soul to know what is good for us, we can find far greater fulfilment. For as long as we are chasing happiness, our souls will never rest and we will never find it. If we remain still and quiet amidst our noisy minds and frantic bodies, if we look inwards, if we reconnect with ourselves and with the natural world around us then we will find peace. And only in finding peace will we find true and lasting happiness.

MANTRA for the soul: I love and accept myself completely.

Reflection: Sit or lie down quietly in a place where you feel safe and comfortable. Think about an area of your life that you are not satisfied with or something that does not bring you happiness. Be honest with yourself about this. It may be something that you find difficult to acknowledge but be courageous and identify it. Give it a name. Now think about how that thing in your life makes you feel. What would you be and how would you be without it? What would be different? How would not having to manage that change your life? Are there negative as well as positive outcomes? Overall, would the change be a positive or a negative one? What are your fears about making the change? What are the challenges? What is stopping you from making that change for yourself? Now change your focus slightly to your life after the change. What does it look like? How do you feel in a life without this negative aspect in it? How has it affected other parts of your life and wellbeing? If this is a positive experience for you, spend some time thinking about whether you feel that you deserve this new, happier life? Is your feeling of self-worth holding you back from making changes that would leave you more fulfilled and happy? If so, this is an area that really needs urgent attention. Make the change: you deserve every happiness.

Exercise: Write down five things that bring you a feeling of peace and contentment. Write down five things that bring you a feeling of joy.

Notice where the lists overlap and where they differ. Write down why you think that some things bring you peace and not joy and vice versa and why some things bring you both.

Chapter 14
The Next Generation

The next generation is living in what is perhaps the most challenging social environment yet. They are constantly being drawn into the virtual world of social media, much of which places great importance on material possessions, external beauty and validation from strangers. In school, they are limited in their ability to be creative and individual. Resistance against conformity is discouraged and they face a constant stream of testing and comparison against the results of their peers. Their individuality and unique spark disappears. When coupled with the monumental challenge that the next generation faces in halting the destruction of our natural world, the pressure really is mounting upon our children today.

We know that the instance of mental health problems in young people is growing year after year, at a time when the availability of mental health services is reducing. Mental health problems affect about one in ten children and young people. They include depression, anxiety, eating disorders and self-harm as well as conduct disorders and are often a direct response to what is happening in their lives. Alarmingly, however, 70% of children and young people who experience a mental health problem have not had appropriate interventions at a sufficiently early age. This is simply not good enough when we consider that the emotional wellbeing of children is just as important as their physical health. It is a frightening statistic that in the UK, one in eight of 17- to 19-year-old girls have self-harmed or attempted suicide. There is a 90% increase in number of students experiencing anxiety or stress in recent years; 81% of pupils would like their school to teach them more about their mental health; 80% of young people say that exam pressure has significantly impacted their mental health; 75% of mental health problems are established by age 18 and 50% by age 14; 25% of 14-year-old girls across the UK are clinically depressed. These figures will undoubtedly have become more troubling still as a result of the COVID19 pandemic. This cannot go on.

Good mental health allows children and young people to develop the resilience to cope with whatever life throws at them and grow into well-rounded, healthy adults. There are a number of simple measures that can keep our children and young people mentally well including:

- Being in good physical health, eating a balanced diet and getting regular exercise
- Having time and the freedom to play, indoors and outdoors
- Being part of a family that gets along well most of the time
- Going to a school that looks after the wellbeing of all its pupils
- Taking part in local activities for young people.

- Helping them to feel loved, trusted, understood, valued and safe
- Encouraging them to be interested in life and create opportunities to enjoy themselves
- Supporting them to be hopeful and optimistic
- Enabling them to able to learn and having opportunities to succeed
- Guiding them to accept and value who they are and to recognise what they are good at
- Generating a sense of belonging in their family, school and community
- Showing them that they have some control over their own life
- Developing with them the strength to cope when something is wrong (resilience) and the ability to solve problems.

It is true that these factors are important but keeping children well requires them to hold and maintain a genuine sense of empowerment over their lives and their futures. Children and young people must learn to identify with their resilience if they are to stay well and fulfil their potential in the face of so many life challenges.

There is so much that we can do to help them. We can teach them the importance of controlling their thought processes to develop a life based in reality and truth rather than in ego and judgment. We should encourage them to stay true to who they genuinely are, resisting the powerful influence of peer pressure and social media and to be a voice, not an echo. We can help them to feel satisfied with who they are and what they have by teaching them the importance of a positive mind-set and by helping them understand that everything they need to live meaningfully is inside of them already. We must remind them that they are valuable individuals with a completely unique and specific purpose and skillset which cannot be compared to others. We can educate them to strive only to fulfil their own potential and not to strive to meet expectations set by others or to seek validation from outside of themselves. We should give them confidence in their instinct, to trust that instinct, to guide them towards what is comfortable for them and away from what is not and to always trust and believe in that. We must teach them to stay connected to their physical selves and to fully process trauma and to have the wisdom to seek out support willingly and easily and without shame.

We must help our children to develop a reliable resilience framework of support and trust of which they are an intrinsic part and within which they give back to others. We should promote their self-confidence and belief in themselves; belief that they have worth and importance and a voice. We can build communities to which they can belong and which are mutually beneficial to all members. We have to shine a light on their responsibilities as well as on their rights. We must never let them forget the importance of kindness. We need to teach by example sustainable patterns of wellbeing in physical and mental health, nutrition and sleep and educate them in a genuine understanding of how deficiencies in any area will impact upon their learning and development as well as on their health. We should help them to understand the importance of human connection and of the unending bond they have with our planet, to be grounded in their place in the world.

Our society is often described as 'broken' or fractured, but our children who will control our world in the years to come are whole, they are not yet broken. With the right support and direction, they can and will navigate their way through life's challenges with confidence, making positive and lasting changes to their individual lives and to our planet.

The success that our young people and indeed all of us should be supported to attain cannot be defined or pursued. It is a feeling of satisfaction that comes when the balance is right.

"Success is the result of a more gentle, loving, balanced, caring and connected orientation of the world. The heart knows that there are many environmental factors that are beyond anyone's control. It knows that some life obstacles are put there because they cannot be overcome and because they are there to teach us to stop trying and start being."

The Heart's Code – Paul Pearsall

These lessons combined will create the most fulfilling and self-nurturing community in which our younger generation can 'be' rather than 'do' and can heal and thrive in contentment, wellness, positivity and hope.

MANTRA for young people: Everything I need is already inside of me

ALTR Life:
Worship Yourself: Create Change

Epilogue

Whether you believe that you can or that you cannot, you are right.